100X

100X

10X YOUR RESULTS
USING
10X LESS EFFORT

William U. Peña, MBA

Dedication

To Matthew and Max, my sons, who give me
the best reason to work less, and set the right
priorities in my life.

To my wife, Genie, who put up with me for the last
two decades and is willing to continue.

To my mentor, David Finkel, who gave me the faith
that I could, "Have my cake, and eat it too."

To Peter Diamandis who showed me that anything
is possible with an abundant heart.

And to God, who has been,
and will always be, my friend..

100X

CONTENTS

100X

PREFACE

This book is for entrepreneurs.

But not just any entrepreneurs. This book is for entrepreneurs who know and believe there is a better, faster, easier way to reach our goals in business and life—whether that's making a million, a hundred million, a billion or more.

We know and believe there is a way to cut to the front of the line and avoid all the unnecessary work everyone else is doing.

We don't believe in "get rich quick"—even though we know it's possible. We're more interested in "get rich smart" because we know there is a way to get there 100X faster and with less work compared to everyone else.

We believe in 80/20 and we live it. We believe we can hack anything and everything and get to escape velocity in our goals while everyone else is still taking their first step.

100X

People call us rebels, outliers, eccentrics and renegades, iconoclasts, mavericks and out-of-the-box thinkers. For us, there is no spoon because we don't think in- or out-of-the-box, because to us, there is no box.

We love words like exponential, explosive, catalyst and multiply. As well as words like maximize, democratize, and optimize. We love to disrupt anything in our way. And leverage is our middle name.

We hate words like can't, hard, and difficult, which for us, are just fuel to our fire and provokes us to gear up for the challenge. And we eat the word "impossible" for breakfast.

We build atomic habits because we know they're necessary. We have made peace with incremental growth; though it's still hard to swallow. And we've learned to appreciate the gain, no matter how small—though closing the gap drives us on.

But we play in the playground of the powerful, engage in the arena of the exponential, find amusement in the explosive. And, when it's all said and done, we make the majestic our mansion.

Yes, we work hard and play hard. But we do it shrewdly, making money even while asleep.

One of our favorite Einstein quotes is, "Intelligent people solve problems, but geniuses avoid them." So we strive to be the geniuses, shaping the world as we see fit.

We are Neo, the One, the saviors in the Matrix, who strives to unplug as many people as possible even when we know 99% will

x   x   x

remain the same. But we try anyway because this is what we are made for.

We are the visionaries, the bold, the brash, who dare to set big goals, have a do-or-die mentality and put everything on the line to make them a reality. But we're smart about it, so even if we lose, we always win.

We don't expect 2x results, we laugh at 5X results. Even 10X is beneath us. No, we expect at least 100X results (which is a steppingstone to achieve 1 MillionX results too).

Why?

Because we know we can.

We are the new generation of entrepreneurs.

We are 100X entrepreneurs.

Welcome to our movement.

100X

ARE YOU READY TO GO 100X?

"Entrepreneurs are simply those who understand that there is little difference between
obstacle and opportunity and are able to
turn both to their advantage."
– Niccolo Machiavelli (The Prince)

My name is Will Peña, and I'm an entrepreneur.

I wasn't always an entrepreneur. I worked a full-time job for many years. I've worked as a bus boy, an apartment janitor, a tutor, a barista, a call center agent, and even as an archaeologist assistant at one point. I've been a business consultant helping business owners grow their businesses, and I've even worked as a minister helping people better their lives.

But the one thing that I can say with certainty is that I felt out of place at every one of those jobs. As a matter of fact, I've felt out of place mostly everywhere I've been in life.

100X

Why? Because in my heart, I am an entrepreneur.

You see, life only makes sense to us when we are out in the world upsetting the apple cart, venturing into places we are told not to go, looking for something to break to make it work better, or fixing the problems of the world that no one seems to care about.

Because that is what entrepreneurs do.

The Entrepreneur's Journey

I was born to immigrant parents who came to the United States from the Dominican Republic to escape the umbrella of poverty that eclipsed their lives. My parents immigrated to the United States looking for a better life. My dad, a car mechanic, and my mom, a housewife, brought three of their kids to a country they had never been to before and whose language they didn't speak.

A few years after arriving, my brother was born and, a year after that, another sister, making up a family of seven. Then lo and behold, to their surprise, and exhausted dismay, I was on the way.

What happened after that was just a series of tragedies that would change the course of my family's life forever. A few years into their trip to the US, one of my sisters fell over on her highchair and died. Then, when I was 9 months, my father died of a rare disease at the young age of 30.

So my mother was left to contend with the pain of a dead child from a few years earlier and the heartache of a dead husband. Not to mention five crazy kids who made her life ten times harder. Besides this, she spoke absolutely no English, and didn't even know how to fill out a money order.

To say that my mother had a backbone of steel is an understatement. Besides being a single mom in a country she did not know, she had to raise me (a baby) and my 4 other brothers and sisters on her own. And if that wasn't enough, she also had to contend with poverty, and the violence and dangers of living in Washington Heights in NY during the height of a crime wave.

Humble Beginnings

Life in Washington Heights wasn't as pretty as they portray it on Broadway or in the movies. It was as rough and dangerous as any low socio-economic status environment. The sounds of gunshots and sirens were our bedtime lullaby, and it got to the point that we couldn't go to sleep without them.

Being one of the few lightest-skinned Hispanic boys in a school in the hood wasn't easy either. I would get picked on for being different, and a lot of kids made it pretty clear that I didn't belong. I got bullied, spat on, laughed at, and beat up.

Besides all that, I carried the same feeling throughout my childhood—that I didn't belong. I felt like I didn't belong in my family, neighborhood, or school. I felt like my life was designed for a different purpose, a greater purpose, but I didn't know what it was.

School was especially difficult for me. I felt out of place in the rigid education system because I wanted to be free to learn on my own. I

100X

felt so out of place that I would act out as the class clown, resulting in detention 8 months out of a 10-month school year. I got so used to detention that the Vice Principal of the school and I became great friends. And in all honesty, I think I learned more from her than I did in all my time in school. (Looking back, she reminded me of a young Oprah Winfrey).

I started cutting classes to get through the boring and rote school routine. But I didn't cut class to go to the mall (the closest thing we had to a mall was the bodega on the corner). And I didn't cut class to go paint graffiti on the trains (though it was a hobby I would later pick up to help brighten up the abandoned buildings in our neighborhood). I would cut class and go to the library.

I just felt I needed to learn, and that I wasn't learning anything meaningful in school, so I decided to do it on my own. I'd cut class and go to the library, where I would devour books on anything that interested me. I could tell the librarians wondered why I wasn't at school, but I think they were so encouraged by how much I was reading that they left me alone.

I would drink up all I could learn from every row of books I could find, and every colorful encyclopedia in the reference area they would let me read. This was my YouTube (because, ahem, back then there was no YouTube). I was so eager to learn that I even began to steal books from the library to take home (yeah, I know. But my intentions were good).

What Am I Here For?

When I turned 16, I had an existential crisis, feeling like there was no purpose in life. With no guidance or support, I felt all on my own. It wasn't easy trying to figure out what I was doing on this earth, and what I would do with the rest of the years ahead. It was getting harder to find my purpose in life, and I ultimately concluded that life wasn't worth living, which led me to contemplate suicide on multiple occasions. What saved me was that the more I read, the more I began to believe and hope that there was a role out there just for me. That I just hadn't found it yet. So I pressed on.

I was lucky enough to become part of a great church during this time. They taught me about having a spiritual purpose and I had access to great men who influenced and helped me understand what it meant to be a godly man. That gave me the foundation I needed to become a decent human being, despite the anger, fear, worry, hurt, and anxiety that I had stored up from my childhood.

But even as time went on, I still felt out of place. Even though I was more content with life, I still felt like I had a role to play, like there was a reason I was created. I didn't know what it was yet.

A few years later, I was offered a position to work for a financial firm, and while waiting for the final confirmation (which never came), I decided to test my first attempt at entrepreneurship as a real estate investor. It was the early 2000's, during the housing mania, when they were giving loans to anyone who could breathe. It was so easy to get a loan that I bought 17 houses within 18 months.

100X

Then the housing crisis of 2008 came, and everything evaporated. I lost every house except for 2, which I eventually lost a few years later. So I was back at square one, but I now had 4 million dollars in debt to my name. And even though it was my first experience with entrepreneurship and I had failed, I was hooked.

After tasting the excitement of entrepreneurship, I decided I did not ever want to go back to work for other people. But since I didn't have any business skills, I decided to do the next best thing. I enrolled into grad school because they were giving away free money (aka loans) to attend, and I thought I might learn something. It also gave me at least 2 years when I didn't need to worry about bills, and it was a legitimate excuse I could use to keep the 4-million-dollar debt collectors at bay.

Fast forward to December of 2013, and by this point, I am married and with a 7-year-old son. I had an MBA in international business and was working on a second MBA in International Taxation. With all the financial pressures that came from having a small family, my entrepreneurial resolve broke down and I decided I had to get a job. But because of the financial meltdown, the economy was still in the toilet years later. So no matter how hard I tried, and despite sending out over 100 resumes, I couldn't find a regular job.

To pay the bills, I started working as a part-time business consultant, helping small business owners learn how to grow their businesses. What was funny was that having the "MBA" next to my name made it seem like I knew what I was doing. The truth was, I didn't have a clue what it took to be a successful entrepreneur. So I just tried to use the one talent I did have, which was reading.

My plan was to be two steps ahead of my clients and feed them what I was learning.

An unfortunate pattern in the business consulting world is that client contracts end at the end of the year, and you must go find new ones. So, financial things started to crumble when I lost all my clients at the end of 2014. On top of that, I had only $6 in my bank account, and the rent was due in a few days.

Even after all that I learned about business in my MBA programs, I still couldn't keep enough money in my bank account to keep my wife, son and I afloat. It's like the book *Rich Dad, Poor Dad*—and if you've ever read the book, I was the poor Dad in this situation.

So I had a choice to make between getting evicted (not an option) or going back and mooching from my in-laws (an option filled with shame and embarrassment). Or better yet, find a way to make enough money to pay my rent and bills (did I tell you that they were due in a few days?), and hopefully have a little money left over to start a side business of my own.

I knew there had to be a way to make a few thousand dollars in a few days. I had read enough books and seen enough videos to know it was possible. I just had to figure out what to do, and get it done fast.

So I asked myself what would turn out to be the 100X Question:

> *"How can I 10X my return, while using 10X less time, effort, resources and money?"*

Then it came to me.

100X

I had recently been doing a lot of research on passive income, and I was starting to experiment with the concept. I had read so much about it that by that point; I knew more than most people. And my small experiments had started to show some promise.

So, I decided to put on a Passive Income webinar, and invited everyone I knew, or I had ever done business with to join. Then I decided to sell a 90-Day Passive Income consulting program for $2000 each. Why so much? Because it was enough to pay my rent and I would have some money to start my own little passive income venture. And this way, I could still pay my rent even if only one person signed up.

But one person didn't come.

Twenty people came.

And one person didn't sign up for the program.

Four people signed up for the program, and in a 2-hour presentation, I made $8000.

I went from $6 in my bank account to $8006 dollars in my bank account, all in a span of two hours. I didn't just 10X my return, I got over 1334X on my return. And it only took two hours and a few additional hours weekly to service my new 4 clients.

I was able to more than 10X my return, using 10X less time, effort, resources, and money (what I refer to as TERM)—an idea that eventually came to be called 100X.

Because 10X times 10X = 100X!

x **xx** x

Was it Just a Fluke?

After going through this experience, I was really hooked.

I wondered: "If I could do that in a week, what else could I apply the 100X formula to?"

At the time, I was starting a side business and decided to build it with the 100X philosophy in mind. So I asked the 100X question:

> *"How can I build a business that gives me 10X return while using 10X TERM?"*

I started looking for passive income ideas that fit this bill.

One of the first business ventures I tried was importing and exporting. With $500 to start, I decided to find a product in China of decent quality that was in high demand and sell it in the US. I ended up starting a business selling binoculars to birdwatchers.

And I struck gold.

In just a few short years, that $500 turned into over 25 million dollars in revenue. But the part that was more mind boggling to me was that I only had to work at that business for 15 minutes a day. That's right—only 15 minutes a day, and, at most, 2 hours a week.

Again, I 10X'd my return (actually, it was more like 40,000X), and I was able to do it while using 10X less TERM.

100X

Was it Just Luck?

After trying so many things in my career and not generating the returns I had hoped for, I had become a die-hard skeptic. I thought that this success at best could only be explained by luck.

I decided to run another experiment and do it again. Except this time, I would only use $200 to start and see if I could 100X my results like I did before.

I decided to get into writing and selling books and spend the first $200 on creating a book cover and design for my first book. I would write the book, and I would see if it could generate the 100X+ returns that I experienced before.

To 10X my return, I looked for the most popular books in the market (according to the first page of Amazon) for inspiration. Since I wanted to use 10X less TERM, I decided to write the books that would take the least time and effort but would still be appreciated for their content. So I chose kid's books because kids couldn't care less how pretty the books looked, or even if they had typos—they just wanted to laugh.

Surprisingly, on the first page of Amazon, I found a children's fan-fiction book based on the video game Minecraft that was selling very well. So I bought it, read it, and decided to write a book that would be 10X better.

My son and I collected all the Minecraft jokes we would usually tell each other while playing the game, and we decided to turn it into a funny children's book. It took us five hours to write it, and I took screenshots from the game itself for images. Then I hired someone on Fiverr to design the cover for $20, and on Upwork to design the inside for $100. I edited the book myself to save money (bad idea, but the kids didn't care), and we were done with the book within a few days.

Then, I uploaded the book to Amazon Kindle Publishing, and waited 24 hours and then it was live. We got the book published, but we knew it would take time to get noticed, so my son and I just went back to playing video games.

The next day, we both couldn't believe our eyes. The book had gained almost 200 five-star reviews overnight. And it continued that way for months. And only a few months later, that December, our book hit the first page of Amazon at position number 5.

Over the course of the new year, because the first book had been successful, I just kept writing one book a month. And when I finally decided to stop writing (after book 18), we had secured licensing contracts with publishers around the world—the biggest being Scholastic.

It got to the point that our books were so popular that we were nominated for a Nickelodeon Kid's Choice Award Kid's Choice Award. But more importantly, over a few years, that $200 had generated over 21 million dollars in revenue and is still making money to this day.

But again, the most impactful part was not the return, but that I only had to work 15 minutes a month to keep that business going. That's right—15 minutes a month.

100X

So again, I 10X'd the return (more like 100,000X), while using 10X less TERM.

As skeptical as I was, after repeating the experience three times, (the webinar, the binocular's company, and the kid's books) it proved to me that there is a world where not only is 100X possible, but it's the norm.

More importantly for me, I had discovered my true calling in life...

I was meant to live the life of a 100X Entrepreneur.

Are You Ready to Go 100X?

This book is designed to show you all the ins and outs of the 100X Entrepreneur's lifestyle—what it is and how you can begin to live the 100X lifestyle and get 100X results as well.

The first part of this book will explore all the reasons that 100X works, the foundational universal principles behind 100X, how powerful 100X truly is, and how the world is abundantly full of 100X opportunities waiting for you to take advantage of.

In the second part, since all major change starts with changing yourself, we will dive into the fundamentals, including how to 100X your mind, character, productivity, and strategy.

In the third part of this book, you will learn how to 100X every major aspect of your business including: how to 100X your startup ideas, competitive advantage, marketing, sales, systems, network, finances, and opportunities.

Is This Book for You?

In all honesty, this book is not for everyone.

For example, if you're the kind of person who thinks 100X is a pipe dream, it doesn't exist, or that it's just another scam, then this book is not for you.

Or, if you're so skeptical that you don't think 100X is even possible (even though being a skeptic I can relate), this book is probably not for you either.

But that's ok. That just means more of the lion's share of 100X benefits and rewards will be left for the rest of us.

On the other hand, if you not only know that 100X is possible, but you believe that 100X is your destiny, then this book is definitely for you.

Or rather, if you believe that 100X is just a steppingstone to 1000X, 10,000X, 100,000X or even 1 MillionX and more, then consider this book as the universe's stamp of approval, letting you know that you were right all along.

So the only question left to ask yourself is...

Are you ready to go 100X?

If you are, then turn the page and hold onto your seat, because you are about to go where only the bold have gone before.

PART 1

WHAT IS 100X?

WHY 10X IS NOT ENOUGH

"Progress isn't made by early risers. It's made by lazy men trying to find easier ways to do something."
– Robert A. Heinlein

If you haven't read the book "The 10X Rule" by Grant Cardone, then you need to.

It's a manifesto reminding us to stop thinking small. Instead, it challenges us to add a zero to every goal we have, ratchet up our goals to humongous levels, and blow the limits off our thinking. It calls us to not only stop thinking small, but to never live small again. It challenges us to go after the biggest giant, fight the mightiest beast and slay the biggest dragon you can find.

And it's a great testament to Grant Cardone's life.

A Hero's Journey

Born in Lake Charles, Louisiana, Grant Robert Cardone faced the tragedies of life early, losing his father, Curtis Louis Cardone, when he was only ten years old. This devastating loss left him without a crucial male role model during the most important years of his life.

This early experience also taught him harsh realities about money and control, as he watched his mother struggle financially in her efforts trying to manage their household alone.

Raised by a single mother who was responsible for seven children, Cardone grew up in a household that prioritized saving money but was barely scraping by. His mother's focus was on keeping the family afloat, often resorting to clipping coupons and saving every penny. This environment, along with his father's absence, contributed to a sense of uncertainty and a lack of positive influences in his life.

Cardone's teenage years were further disrupted by his drug addiction, beginning as early as 15 years old. He struggled with addiction for over nine years, a period marked by daily drug use and even several overdoses. According to Cardone, lack of self-esteem, boredom, and a lack of vision for his life drove this addiction. The absence of a male figure and positive guidance also played a significant role in his descent into drug abuse.

Despite these challenges, Cardone's journey toward recovery began with a pivotal moment of tough love from his mother. After years of trying to quit drugs and failing, his mother's refusal to enable his addiction led him to seek treatment. He eventually turned his life around, dedicating the time and energy he had spent on drugs to taking massive action and excelling at a job he initially disliked. This shift marked the beginning of his path to rebuilding his self-respect, self-esteem, and ultimately, his career.

Cardone's tough childhood, early struggles with addiction and lack of direction played a massive role in shaping his drive, work ethic, and determination to succeed at all costs. It laid the foundation for his later achievements as a businessman and motivational speaker and laid the foundation for his 10X philosophy for massive achievement.

Why 10X is Not Enough

Cardone's 10X philosophy is based on the idea that if you're going after goals, you may as well 10X those goals and make them as big as possible because no one has ever gotten very far thinking small.

According to Cardone, the way you accomplish these goals is by taking nothing less than massive, herculean action. For example, if you have 50 sales calls to make, don't just make 50, make 500, and give it everything you got in one large-scale push of reckless abandon to accomplish your goal.

As powerful and motivating as it is, the 10X philosophy does have its challenges. The biggest challenge is that it is difficult to maintain a consistent work habit to produce massive results. To consistently keep pushing out that level of work and intensity takes a level of self-discipline that average people just don't have the strength to sustain over time.

In other words, you may have a surge of motivation and discipline to go all out and make 500 sales calls today, but tomorrow, you'll be too exhausted to do it again.

Don't get me wrong: there are some special people (like Grant Cardone) who can keep up that level of intensity going all the time, because it is who they are. And they deserve the rewards the world gives them for their level of intensity and obscene work ethic. But for the rest of us mere mortals, we may be able to do it a few times. Maintaining that kind of work ethic all the time is exhausting.

Or, if we do manage to maintain this level of intensity, we will be too spent to devote anything else to all the other important areas of our lives, like our relationships or even our health. It becomes a zero-sum game, where you expend a massive amount of time, energy, and effort in one 10X spurt, but you have nothing left in the tank for the rest of the areas in your life.

Why 100X is Easier Than 10X

Years ago, I was at a conference taught by my old mentor, David Finkel, and he brought up a theme for us to consider regarding the 10X philosophy. He said:

> **"What if you could go after 10X results, but instead of using massive action, you went after it with massive leverage?"**

In other words, what if you went after 10X results, with 10X less time, effort, resources, and money (TERM)?

So instead of using massive action, which normally means expending an extreme amount of energy, effort, resources, and wherewithal to get results, you replace it with massive leverage. That is through finding creative ways to use less TERM but still get a 10X result or even better.

And the cross-section where 10X results and 10X less effort intersect is where the 100X results are created.

Because 10X times 10X = 100X!

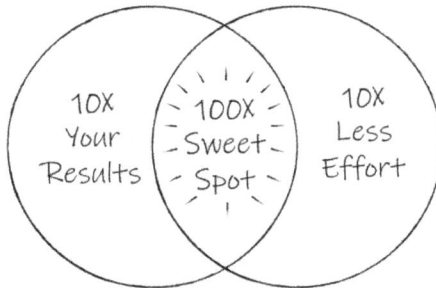

My old mentor used to call it the "sweet spot," which is the inter-section between a 10X return (home run), and 10X less TERM (low hanging fruit).

Leverage is a 4-letter word (TERM)

> "Give me a lever long enough and a fulcrum on which to place it, and I shall move the world."
> **– Archimedes**

In physics, the word leverage relates to a lever's power that allows you to move a large load with a relatively small amount of force. For

Archimedes, the longer the lever, the more load you can lift with an even smaller force.

In business, leverage is associated with going after the big payday without putting any of your resources at risk. A common business example is using financial leverage, aka, borrowing other people's money (OPM). You borrow the money at a low cost to you (interest) then turn around and use that money to buy a house, a business, or inventory. And then either sell it for a profit or you can let those assets appreciate (real estate or business) for a large payday in the future. This is a perfect example of getting a big 10X return (profit and equity) while using 10X less of your TERM.

Therefore, if you can get 10X results using 10X less TERM, why bother using massive action? Why choose massive action when you could achieve the same result much quicker, easier and with less risk?

It's like if you had to take a trip from NY to California. To get there, you have several options: you can walk, use a horse and buggy, bike, drive, take a train, or fly. All these options will take you to your destination. But which one will get you there with the least amount of time and effort? In other words, why choose massive action like walking or taking a bike when you can fly there in a fraction of the time? (And as of writing this book, supersonic jets have just come back in fashion, making the trip even faster).

This book aims to show you that leverage isn't only limited to taking flights to California from NY or borrowing money. Instead, I want to reveal to you that there are hundreds and even thousands more opportunities you could take advantage of to get a 10X return using 10X less TERM. Here are just a few:

1. **Operational Leverage:** Consistently reduce costs in your business operations, so that you can generate more significant profit margins. As sales increase, your costs will constantly decrease, substantially multiplying your ROI.
2. **Leverage through Networking:** Build and maintain an extensive network of influential contacts who can provide access to new opportunities, information, and resources that will lead to a huge exponential jump in results.
3. **Technological Leverage:** Use of technology to improve efficiency and productivity. AI, automation, software tools, and digital platforms are examples where technology creates leverage by doing more with less.
4. **Time Leverage:** Effective time management strategies, such as elimination, automation, delegation, simplification, and the use of productivity tools, help you achieve more in less time.
5. **Knowledge Leverage:** Being a continual learner and using one's knowledge to make better decisions, solve problems more efficiently, and create opportunities.
6. **Emotional Leverage:** Use emotional intelligence skills to build stronger relationships, make better decisions, and maintain a powerful culture.
7. **Physical Leverage**: Invest in your health and wellness to ensure that your physical state supports and helps you better achieve your personal and professional goals.

Ultimately, the more you take advantage of these opportunities in your life and business, the more you can have your cake (10X results) and eat it too (10X less TERM) = 100X!

The Benefits of 100X

Benefits of Using Less Time

If you can achieve your goals using less time, then this would mean more time to:

- **Focus on more important things** in your business.
- **Run your organization more efficiently**, giving you an edge on your competition. **Take care of the other important things in your life**, like your relationships or your health because you'll be working less.

If you go after 10X with massive action, you'll have less time. But if you go after 10X with massive leverage (10X less TERM), you'll have more time, and with that, more freedom.

This is what I experienced when I could run one company working only 15 minutes a day and manage the other company working 15 minutes a month. The extra time I had on my hands gave me the freedom to do a lot of other things I was interested in, and really gave me a great quality of life. It allowed me to have my cake (10X return) and eat it too (10X less time and effort).

Benefits of Using Less Effort

How about achieving your goals with less effort? If you can reach your goal using fewer steps or less work, you can use your extra effort to focus on more valuable areas in your business. Or you can use that effort to multiply your returns by scaling your business. Or maybe start that new business you always wanted to start.

Working less will also mean you'll be more motivated and happier because you won't feel exhausted all the time. You'll have plenty of time to accomplish all that you need to get done because there will be fewer things to complete.

Benefits of Using Less Resources

Even more exciting is reaching your goals using fewer resources or less money. This will mean a bigger profit for you, and a greater return on investment (ROI). Having a higher cashflow to run your business will further increase the value of your business—in case you're thinking of selling it one day in the future. But my favorite part of getting more profits is that you'll be able to put more money into your pocket to take home to the family.

Conclusion

In conclusion, Grant Cardone's 10X principle is a powerful philosophy that can really take you to another level in your business and life. Yet, by itself, it has its limitations because the massive effort it requires is very difficult to maintain.

But what if you could achieve 10X results, but instead of using massive action to achieve it, you apply massive leverage? Meaning, instead of multiplying your time, energy, and effort to get to your goal, you creatively find a way to get to that goal using 10X less TERM.

The benefits of living this way will revolutionize your business and your life. From:

- Having more time for the most important things in your life, like your relationships and your health.
- Using less effort to achieve the same goals, which will improve the quality of your life.
- And, getting to your goals using less resources and money, which will mean more profits, more value for your business and more money to take home to your family.

This is the essence of 100X. **Where 10X results meets massive 10X leverage, and the sweet spot that is created when these two intersect is where the 100X results are born.**

100X isn't a rare occurrence; it is a part of nature as fixed as gravity. And because of this, it will always reward those who jump on that current. Like swimming with the current, when you tap into 100X movement, you will see mind-blowing and very profitable results in your business and life.

It happened to me, and it can happen to you as well.

But if you're not convinced, turn the page, and let's talk about the universal principles that are the foundational drivers for making 100X a reality.

ACTION STEPS

Here are some action steps to get you started on your journey to 100X:

1. List three times when you've experienced huge results and it only took a little TERM on your part.
2. What are some sweet spot opportunities you can take advantage of right now, that can give you big results (home run) with little TERM (low hanging fruit)?

PRINCIPLES OF 100X

"An army of principles can penetrate where an army of soldiers cannot."
– Thomas Paine

In 1873, a visionary writer, named Jules Verne published a book called, "Around the World in Eighty Days." One of Verne's most famous works, this novel reflected the technological advancements and global curiosity of the time.

In the book, Verne's hero, Phileas Fogg, accepts a wager to complete a journey around the world in eighty days, a task that seemed impossible at the time.

The story reflected the era's fascination with exploration, adventure, and the capabilities of modern technology—a theme that has inspired entrepreneurs throughout history.

It was such a motivating book, in fact, that it inspired Sir Richard Branson to take on the same challenge and attempt to circumnavigate the globe in a hot air balloon.

In 1987, Branson made his first attempt at ballooning across the Atlantic but ended up in the water. In 1991, he became the first to cross the Pacific Ocean in a balloon. In 1998, Branson attempted the first non-stop journey around the globe but he had to abandon the mission in Hawaii due to fuel shortages and technical issues. And, in December 1999, Branson made another attempt, but once again, had to abort his mission in Hawaii due to a torn envelope and severe weather conditions.

And although he broke many records, Branson never made it.

But, in 2002, Steve Fossett, one of Branson's previous teammates, attempted to travel around the world in a hot air balloon as well. Except this time, he did something that had never been done before—he did it alone.

So, on June 19, 2002, he launched the Spirit of Freedom balloon from Northam, Western Australia. Then, on July 2, 2002, Fossett landed in Queensland, Australia, successfully circumnavigating the globe, but not in 80 days.

He completed the entire journey in 14 days, 19 hours, and 50 minutes.

Easy and Effortless

How did Fossett accomplish the feat of circumnavigating the globe when Branson, and many others who had tried before, did not?

A major reason for Fossett's success was because he relied on leverage, with a little help from Mother Nature, to do most of the work for him.

You see, Fossett, like Branson, had unsuccessfully tried to accomplish this feat many times before. But, learning from his previous failures, he used the latest technology more wisely, and managed risks more effectively. More importantly, making the decision to travel alone reduced the complexities of the trip and the balloon's weight. This allowed Fossett to harness the immense power of high-altitude wind currents and the jet streams more effectively. By riding these powerful winds, Fossett's balloon achieved significantly higher speeds, allowing him to cover great distances in a shorter amount of time.

It's kind of like the movie finding Nemo. In the movie, Nemo's dad, Marlin, jumps on the East Australian Current (EAC) to get to Sydney to find Nemo. He could've swum to Sydney, but instead, by jumping on the EAC, and surfing on a turtle's back, he took the expressway all the way to Sydney to find his son.

By deciding to travel light, Fossett effectively leveraged the earth's currents, which allowed him to go a greater distance, and achieve his goal faster, all with substantially less effort.

The Power of Universal Principles

This is a great example that shows how there are universal principles in this world that are at the heart of how the world flows and works. And these principles have powerfully moved the world for thousands of years, and they will continue to influence the world for thousands of years after we're gone.

Gravity is an example of a universal scientific principle that governs nature. If you stepped off a mountain a thousand years ago, you would have fallen and broken your keister, just like you would if you were to step off a mountain today.

There are other types of universal principles called, psycho-social universal principles, that govern how humans relate to themselves and others. And since business relies on these interpersonal relationships, if you rely on these universal psycho-social principles, they will greatly help you get to where you want to go in business.

A great example of this is the principle of building rapport. The principle states that if you first take the time and make an effort to build rapport and trust in a relationship, your influence in the relationship grows substantially. This principle alone can determine the outcome of a sale, or whether you're able to win back an irate customer.

If you've been running into challenges building your business and you don't know why, keep getting inconsistent results, or feel like the ride toward your goals feels more like a roller coaster instead of a rocket ship, then it's likely because you are swimming against these universal psycho-social principles, instead of with them.

So let's dive in and discover the universal principles that make 100X possible, so that you can jump on the back of your turtle, hop onto the current, and catch the expressway to reach your financial goals.

The Pareto Principle (aka: The 80/20 Rule)

The Pareto Principle, also known as the 80/20 Rule, is named after Italian economist Vilfredo Pareto who observed in 1906 that 80% of the land in Italy was owned by 20% of the population. He also observed the same pattern in many other aspects of the natural world and began to identify the universality of this phenomenon.

Later, business management specialist, Joseph Juran, discovered the same principle in manufacturing, observing that most problems (80%) are often produced by a small number of causes (20%). He was also the originator of the "Law of the Vital Few" that emphasized that a small number of causes (the vital few) are responsible for a large proportion of the effect.

The 80/20 rule can be found in many areas across the world. It applies to groups of people, animals, agriculture, products, software, data and more. The exact quantity does not matter—it could be 70/30, 95/5, even 60/40. The tendency is for a small portion of the group to produce the greatest impact.

Out of all the universal principles, there is no better principle that is at the heart of 100X Thinking than the 80/20 rule. This is because 100X is just an extension of the 80/20 rule itself.

100X is based on the idea that you can generate 10X returns (80%) while using 10X less time, effort, resources, and money (20%).

So living by 100X means focusing on only doing the most impactful 20% areas of your business. And by doing this, you will produce the 80% lion's share of results.

Ockham's Razor

Ockham's Razor is a principle that originated from a 14th century logician and Franciscan friar named William of Ockham. When applied to business, the principle simply translates to, "the simplest solution is usually the best solution."

You would assume that keeping things simple would be common sense. But I, like many other entrepreneurs, tend to complicate the simplest things, resulting in a massive use of time, effort, resources, and money (TERM), all to get a small return.

100X Thinking is understanding that since the **simplest solution is the best solution,** then there is always an opportunity to get your desired result by finding simpler and less costly ways of doing it. So, 100X Thinking means dedicating yourself to using Ockham's "razor" to constantly shave off unnecessary time, effort, and resources, while striving to get a better return. The result is that you'll get a greater return on investment because more is being created with fewer resources.

Parkinson's Law

Cyril Northcote Parkinson first described the principle of Parkinson's Law. It states that, "work expands so as to fill the time available for its completion." In other words, the amount of time you set aside to perform a task will eventually equal the amount of time that it takes you to complete that task.

We've all experienced this phenomenon. A good example is if you've ever had to write a term paper in high school. I know I procrastinated and ended up writing the paper last minute. And because I had only one day left to turn in the term paper, I would miraculously get it done in that one day—even though the teacher gave me 2 weeks to finish it. This shows us that it only takes 1 day to complete the term paper, but I spent the entire 2 weeks wasting time and effort stressing about it.

You may have experienced this as an entrepreneur. If you've ever had a day where you spent the entire day working, but then you felt like you didn't get very much done at the end of the day, then you know what I'm talking about.

What causes this? Parkinson's Law. Like water that fills whatever container you put it in, when we don't put limits on ourselves, we will just fill up whatever time or spend away whatever budget we set out for ourselves.

100X Thinking takes advantage of Parkinson's Law because the opposite is also true. Meaning, if we put smaller time limits on the work we need to accomplish, we will find that we could finish all our work within that short timeframe.

For example, having a shorter timeframe forces us to focus on doing the most valuable and important tasks, as well as forcing us to delegate or eliminate work that is not as valuable. The result is that you get 10X more done, using 10X less effort.

Therefore, operating by 100X means constantly putting tighter and tighter **limits on your TERM,** forcing you to achieve your goals and waste less valuable resources, leading you to a 10X greater ROI.

Kaizen

Kaizen, the Japanese word for "improvement," refers to the philosophy that focuses on continuously improving the systems in any business.

Simply, the principle of Kaizen describes two main ideas: 1) There is always room for improvement, and 2) people have a natural tendency to waste resources.

Kaizen suggests that, even if you're getting good results for your current efforts, the opportunity always exists to get better. So dedicating the time and effort to improve will greatly multiply your results. In other words, continuous small improvements will result in exponentially greater results.

Human beings also tend to waste valuable resources. We tend to put in a certain level of input but not receive an equal level of output because our resources get wasted somewhere along the line, and we can never get them back.

This is the biggest reason most entrepreneurs end up working twice as hard but taking home less and less money. Like a laundry machine that sucks up socks and underwear into a black hole never to be seen again, our resources get depleted month after month, and we wonder why we're not getting ahead as fast as we'd hoped.

100X Thinking makes it a priority to invest the time and effort toward continual improvement, knowing that small improvements in our business will result in a greater and greater return on our investment. This means continually finding ways to keep reducing our TERM while simultaneously tweaking our efforts so that it multiplies our return 10X, 60X or 100X.

For example, the idea behind an MVP (minimum viable product) is to spend the least amount of time and money to create a raw prototype, so you can test it as fast as possible in the market-place. Then you get valuable feedback from customers, allowing you to keep improving the product to get closer to what the customers really want. This way, when you release the product, you'll have a much greater chance of your product being a hit instead of a dud.

Or imagine applying the concept of Kaizen to marketing. Before spending money on marketing, first test your marketing using free or inexpensive marketing tactics, tweaking it little by little until you get great results. Then, once the fire is lit, only then do you throw kerosene on it (big money). This way, you have a better chance of getting a great return on our marketing dollars, while minimizing wasted resources.

Conclusion

These few but powerful universal principles are the foundation that drive how the world flows and works. They are also the main drivers behind getting the 100X results that we will discuss later in this book. By aligning yourself with them, they will do all the heavy lifting, and you will be able to reach your goal quicker and with greater results.

100X Thinking is the ultimate extension of these principles because they call you to:

- **80/20**: Focus your efforts on the 20% that brings 80% of results.
- **Parkinson's Law**: Continually limit the amount of time or money spent on accomplishing a task or project to be more efficient.
- **Ockham's Razor**: Shave off unnecessary work or steps in search of simpler solutions.
- **Kaizen**: Invest time in continual improvement, and reduce waste, because by doing so, you will produce 100X results in terms of revenue, profits, and freedom.

100X Thinking at its core is just aligning yourself with the universal principles that have existed long before we got here. So if you choose the 100X lifestyle—like Steve Fosset did during his solo trip around the world, or like Marlin the clownfish did in his journey to find Nemo—not only will you go longer, and farther, but you will get to your goals quicker, easily, and effortlessly.

For the 100X thinker, getting 100X returns is not only possible, but inevitable, because universal principles are the driving force behind them. And the lion's share of powerful rewards will be waiting for you on the other side, as the next chapter will explain in detail.

ACTION STEPS

1. Do a review of your business and ask:

   a. **80/20 Rule:** What is the 20% that is generating 80% of the return in my business?

   b. **Ockham's Razor:** What are some steps I can remove from what I currently do?

   c. **Parkinson's Law:** What time and spending limits can I put on myself, so that I get more done with less?

   d. **Kaizen:** What are some small improvements that I can make in my business?

THE POWER OF 100X

"Exploration is really the essence of the human spirit."
— Frank Borman, Astronaut commander of Apollo 8

In 2012, a television show called Revolution was released, showing what life would be like if, suddenly, all electricity was gone.

Even though it wasn't quality television, the background story was intriguing. In the show, a hundred quadrillion nanites in the atmosphere absorbed all the electricity, leaving nothing for the world to use.

The result? Life became dismal, reverting back to 1800s style living, with horse and carriage, fighting with swords, cooking over fire, and only working when the sun was out. It gave a glimpse of how different life was compared to today.

What is amazing is that back in the 1800s, one man's small invention led people out of this dismal lifestyle and completely transformed the world as we know it. That man was Thomas Edison, and his invention was a little product called the light bulb.

Though a small, compact, and simple invention, the lightbulb was responsible for adding over 204 trillion man hours of work to the world and changed life as we know it. And this doesn't account for all the other ideas generated from this lightbulb moment (Pun intended).

What is probably most interesting about Edison's invention is that he didn't invent it. The lightbulb, or a form of it, had been around for 80 years before Edison even began experimenting with it.

So imagine this: there was an opportunity that would have had an explosive impact all over the world—with the potential to generate obscene amounts of money for whoever would find it—but no one noticed for 80 years.

But how did Thomas Edison find it?

Because he was looking for it.

This is a perfect example of how curious men and women can harness the power of 100X.

100X Power

The power of 100X is the idea that there are abundant opportunities in the world today that are full of unimaginable power that could change the world and make you wealthy. Not only are they abundant, but these ideas are right in front of our faces—ripe for the picking for anyone brave enough, determined enough and creative enough to go looking for them.

In other words, there are abundant opportunities everywhere that could easily change your life today and could quickly put you in a completely different financial tax bracket. There are even more abundant opportunities like these for your business, which could help you put it on a path to getting 100X returns, and maybe even help you change the world in the process.

The best part is that, like the invention of the lightbulb, some of these 100X opportunities come in very small packages, and you only need a very little amount of time, effort, resources, and money (TERM) to capture them.

Think about some of the simple, life-changing historical inventions that have changed the world:Inventions like Johannes Gutenberg's printing press that revolutionized how we distributed and consumed information Or James Watt's steam engine that revolutionized the use of power for travel. Also, there's the internal combustion engine made commonplace by Henry Ford. All these inventions have changed the world, and were available for anyone to discover and develop if they were searching for them and had the guts to act and persevere until they created something useful.

Don't believe me? Consider that currently all these inventions can be found in the typical 8th-grade science classroom. In other words, anyone could've invented them. If only they were searching for them.

And although today's inventions like the television, computers, the internet, social media, and AI, seem incomprehensible, I don't think it will be a stretch of the imagination to believe that in 50 years, you'll find all these in an 8th grade science class as well.What I am saying is that there is an abundance of powerful 100X opportunities, in plain sight, right in front of our faces, and you don't need to be a rocket scientist to discover them or take advantage of them. You just need to look.

Let me give you an example:

When I was building my binocular business, hunters were the biggest market for the product. Then one day, I decided to read the thousands of product reviews to get a better understanding of my customers' needs.

I discovered that there were hundreds of birdwatchers leaving reviews requesting the specs for the binoculars to be changed to fit the needs of birdwatchers. Birdwatchers needed different specs, like a wide view, close focus, and lightweight features, compared to what hunters needed (long-distance view).

I found out that the birdwatchers were buying our binoculars because the only other birdwatching manufacturer was charging a minimum of $2000 to get a good pair of binoculars specially designed for birdwatching. This was completely out of the budget for the backyard birdwatchers who made up 80% of the birdwatching market.

So I found this untapped opportunity, mind you, that was sitting right in front of me, easily within my reach (if I had bothered to read our reviews earlier), and no one in the world was doing anything about it.

So, I decided to do something about it. I changed our entire business model to service only birdwatchers. I contacted our manufacturer to change all the specs of our binoculars to give birdwatchers exactly what they needed. Then I charged prices in the low $100's so that it would be in their price range.

The result was that our sales skyrocketed. That year, we had our first month selling 1 million dollars of binoculars in one month. Then our brand became known all over the world as the "go to" budget birdwatching binocular with excellent quality.

Here was just another example where the 100X opportunity was in plain sight, but I and the entire marketplace had missed it. But once I tapped into it, it quickly produced 100X the result.

Seek and You Will Find

Have you ever gone shopping for something specific like a car, watch, or a type of jewelry, then somehow, suddenly, you notice it everywhere?

This comes from a phenomenon called the "Frequency Illusion." This happens when something you've recently noticed, learned about, or thought about, suddenly seems to appear everywhere in your daily life.

It isn't that these items are appearing more often, but rather, you've developed a heightened awareness of them because you've tapped into your "selective attention." Once you notice a new car, watch, or piece of jewelry, your brain seems to be on the lookout for it, and you become more likely to notice it when it appears again. This is part of your brain's natural tendency to recognize patterns and familiar things.

The good news is that you can use this feature to your advantage. If the world is filled with powerful 100X opportunities, then the more you search for them, the more your brain will be trained to find them. But the opposite is also true. If you are not searching for these opportunities, then you will train your brain to ignore them—even though they could be right in front of your face. This is the state that most people, and some entrepreneurs, find themselves in every day.

So if your business is stagnant right now, you are growing incrementally at a snail's pace, or the gap to getting to your financial goals is getting larger and larger, it's probably because you are missing the powerful 100X opportunities that are right in front of you. And, this is most likely happening to you because you've not made the effort to search for them.

But if you want to begin to 100X your results, then you need to be on the lookout daily for 100X opportunities.

Finding 100X Opportunities

A great place to start looking for 100X opportunities is in your backyard—look at what you are already doing and think about ways to repurpose what you have to 10X your return using 10X less time, effort, resources and money (TERM).

Reflection Checkpoint

Here are some great questions to ask yourself to help you find more 100X opportunities:

1. Ask the 10X Repurpose Question:
   a. How can I repurpose what I am doing, so that it gives me a 10X bigger return, and a much greater impact?

Asking this question will jumpstart your mind to find creative ways to get 10X more than what we are settling for.

Examples of this could include: charging higher prices, or upselling higher-priced items to more customers.

2. Ask the 10X Leverage Question
   a. How can I eliminate, automate, delegate, or simplify (EADS) what I am doing so I can use 10X less TERM?

This question helps you identify ways to do things with fewer steps, less money, using different strategies, and accomplishing them faster and easier.

Examples of this could include: removing steps from your current system, cutting your expenses by 50%, or working with fewer customers (i.e.: only working with high-value customers and firing the rest).

Then put them together and you get 10X times 10X or 100X!

Let me give you an example of how this works:

When I was looking for an exercise program to build muscle, I searched for an exercise regimen that could help me build a lot of muscle while using the least amount of work involved. It's not that I'm lazy, but after living the 100X lifestyle, I knew there was a better way to gain a lot of muscle with less time and effort.

Most weight training programs require going to the gym at least three times a week and working out for 45 minutes to 1 hour, which didn't fit my criteria. So I kept looking.

As the good book says: "Seek, and you will find." So, a short time after, I found a book that described the idea of putting variable resistance instead of fixed resistance on your muscles to help them get stronger.

It gave the background science that describes how most weight training regimens don't work because the weight you start at a resting stage is useless to build muscle at the strongest stage of your movement (think pushing a weight from your chest [resting stage] to extending your arms fully [strongest stage]). So you are putting in a lot of effort but getting only 50% benefit. But you could build muscle a lot faster if you put the right amount of increasing weight throughout the entire weightlifting range of motion (variable resistance).

So I found a system that used industrial strength rubber bands (600lbs of pressure) to create variable resistance throughout your entire weightlifting movement. I incrementally put more resistance on my muscles as I moved from my resting stage to my strongest stage.

After a month of testing, the results were jaw-dropping. I was able to build more muscle in a month of working out and got better results than I had ever received lifting weights my entire life.

And the best part? I only had to do it for 10 minutes a day.

So I got a 10X result (more muscle, lower body fat, and more strength), using 10X less time and effort (10 minutes a day). 100X!

There is No Spoon

100X opportunities are in plain sight, but most people are oblivious to them—mainly because they aren't searching for them. Most people are stuck in slow growth mode, and they don't realize that there are exponential and explosive opportunities easily available to them. All they have to do is make the effort to search for them, a skill which I am going to teach you in this book.

The biggest reason I think entrepreneurs don't make the effort to search for 100X opportunities is that it usually takes creativity and stepping out-of-the-box to even see these opportunities. It calls us to stop being 2-dimensional, but instead, begin thinking 3-dimensionally, or even 4-dimensionally.

It reminds me of the dialogue from the movie "The Matrix," between Neo and the Spoon Boy:

Spoon Boy: "Do not try and bend the spoon. That's impossible. Instead... only try to realize the truth."
Neo: "What truth?"

Spoon Boy: "There is no spoon."

Neo: "There is no spoon?"

Spoon Boy: "Then you'll see that it is not the spoon that bends, it is only yourself."

In other words, when we can flexibly bend ourselves to believe that there are 100X opportunities all around us, then we will find them.

But, it will take rising above the layers of negative attitudes like: "that's impossible" attitude; or the bureaucratic "we don't do that here", or the "if that were true everyone would be doing it" mindset. It's going to mean being the believer, when no one else believes, because in their 2-dimensional minds, they can't comprehend that there is a 3rd or 4th dimension.

It's also going to take an attitude to not accept things as they are, but be willing to break things, repurpose things, rearrange their order, reform them, and make them do things they weren't designed to do.

My favorite example of this being the modern air fryer. People have been frying with oil for thousands of years, but no one in all that time ever thought that they could fry food without using oil. Then in 2005, Fred van der Weij, a Dutch inventor, thought, "why don't we just fry without oil?" So he repurposed what was already there, and then voila! The Air Fryer was born. Now it has created an air fryer market worth over 1 billion dollars and growing.

It's like the famous quote by George Bernard Shaw that says:

> "The reasonable man adapts himself to the world; the unreasonable one persists in trying to adapt the world to himself. Therefore all progress depends on the unreasonable man."

Now am I saying that finding 100X opportunities be easy? No, but not because they're scarce. It just takes creativity and thinking outside the box because society and our own limits prevent us from seeing the opportunities right in front of our faces.

But if you are willing to believe and search, then it won't be a matter of "if" you will find these powerful 100X opportunities, but a question of "when."

Conclusion

Our world is full of powerful opportunities that can revolutionize our lives, our world, and our financial situation. But even though these opportunities are abundant, many of us miss them because they are hidden in plain sight.

Many people, including some entrepreneurs, don't notice them because they either don't believe they exist, or aren't looking for them. And years can go by before the world sees these opportunities become reality and make the world a better place for everyone.

But the bravest enough, the most determined enough, those creative enough, and the craziest enough, will search for them and will find them. And only they will experience the abundant spoils that will change their life and the world forever.

This is the life of the 100X entrepreneur. And if you're willing to take the next step and explore what it takes to become one, then buckle your seat and get ready for Part 2 of this book.

Part 2 of this book will explore what it takes to 100X yourself so you can 100X your results.

ACTION STEPS

1. **Ask the 10X Repurpose Question:**
   a. How can I repurpose what I am doing, so that it gives me a bigger 10X return, and a much greater impact?

2. **Ask the 10X Leverage Question**
   a. How can I eliminate, automate, delegate, or simplify (EADS) what I am doing, to do it with 10X less effort?

PART 2

100X YOURSELF

100X YOUR MIND

"The mind is the limit. As long as the mind can envision the fact that you can do something, you can do it, as long as you really believe 100 percent."
– Arnold Schwarzenegger

A series of Italian movies portraying the hero Hercules, starring bodybuilders turned actors, became a box office success in the 1950's and 60's. Known as the sword and sandal genre, these movies were so well received in Europe that they were distributed around the world with even more success.

The bodybuilding actors, including Steve Reeves and Reg Park, became some of the most influential leading men during their time. They inspired a revolution in fitness, as many men and young boys aspired to be muscular heroes like the iconic characters portrayed by these actors.

Their beefy, muscular bodies even inspired many famous actors to beef up and become action stars, including Lou Ferrigno (The Hulk), Sylvester Stallone (Expendables), and more.

Their influence was so vast that it even reached the most remote places. In Thal, Styria, a small village near Graz, Austria, a gangly young man would dedicate his life to becoming a bodybuilder after watching one of these films.

But he didn't just decide to become a bodybuilder. This teenager, from a remote rural town, decided he was going to become the greatest bodybuilder in the world.

His name is Arnold Schwarzenegger, and he made history from that day on:

1965 Junior Mr. Europe: Age 18
1966 Best Built Man of Europe: Age 19
1966 Mr. Europe: Age 19
1967 NABBA Mr. Universe (Amateur): Age 20
1968 NABBA Mr. Universe (Professional): Age 21
1968 German Powerlifting Championship: Age 21
1969 IFBB Mr. Universe (Amateur): Age 22
1969 NABBA Mr. Universe (Professional): Age 22
1970 NABBA Mr. Universe (Professional): Age 23
1970 Mr. Olympia: Age 23
1971 Mr. Olympia: Age 24
1972 Mr. Olympia: Age 25
1973 Mr. Olympia: Age 26
1974 Mr. Olympia: Age 27

1975 Mr. Olympia: Age 28
1982–2002: Movie Action Star
2003–2011: Governor of California

How did this skinny young man from a rural village of a few thousand people become one of the most influential men in the world?

Because he believed he could.

Arnold Schwarzenegger was driven by the expectation that he would achieve greatness and nothing else. His reality distortion field changed everything around him to fit his expectations, and he was determined to fulfill them at all costs.

This expectation drove Schwarzenegger to do the things that would lead to his success. Since he expected to be the best, he decided to train with the best and surrounded himself with the champions of the bodybuilding world. He also decided he would be the best in the world, so he did everything in his power to move to where the world champions were located, which was the United States.

And since he expected to beat the best, and to dominate his competitors, he trained harder, had more discipline, and was highly focused on improving any weakness that would give him the edge. In a very short time, he became the GOAT (greatest of all time) in the world of bodybuilding.

You Get What You Expect

Schwarzenegger's big thinking exceeded any limits that could've prevented him from achieving his goals. Any insecurity, hesitation, and limiting beliefs were left behind as he strove to grow and go bigger and bigger. Those limiting beliefs did not have a chance to latch onto his brain because his goals had grown so big that there wasn't any room for limitations to hold him back.

Arnold's expectations became a self-fulfilling prophecy. And his mindset drove his results.

This idea, that you get what you expect, was the basis of an experiment performed in 1964 by an intrepid psychologist named Robert Rosenthal. Rosenthal wanted to find out how our mindset and expectations—and the expectations of those around us—shape our outcomes.

He chose a school called Oak Ridge in South San Francisco for this experiment. Then, with the principal's permission, he told a group of teachers that a specific group of students in their classes were "academic bloomers," and would show significant academic improvement during the year. Then he left the teachers alone to work with the students as usual until the end of the school year when he would test the students.

The reality was that the teachers were given false information. The so-called "academic bloomers" were chosen at random and had been average students up until that point.

The result? By the end of the study, the randomly selected students showed a significant increase in performance, and even their IQ showed greater gains compared to their peers.

Rosenthal successfully proved that our mindset and expectations determine our outcomes.

Yet, this realization leads us to ask ourselves a very important question:

What limits have you put on yourself that are preventing you from doing what you dream of doing, and what you know in your heart you can accomplish?

If you know you were put on this earth to do great things, then what's holding you back?

Before your mind starts filling your head with justifications or excuses, consider this thought for a moment:

If I were to tell you that I would give you 10 Million dollars if you reached all your business goals this year, do you think you would accomplish them?

Or better yet, what if I bumped it up to $100 Million, or even $1 billion? Would you find a way to reach your goals and make them happen? (The negative version of this question would be: If a mafioso threatened to kill everyone you love, unless you reached your business goals this year, would you make it happen?)

If the answer is yes, and I know it is, then why haven't you done it by now?

The answer? It's because of the mental limits you've set for yourself.

Your mindset and expectations are not allowing you to reach your goals. And until you change your mindset and expectations, you will keep pining away at where you want to be and won't be able to get there.

So let me show you how you can break all the boundaries and limits you've put on yourself, and how you can begin to see exponential results in your life and business.

Think 10X Bigger

Schwarzenegger was able to transcend his mental limits because he thought bigger. How much bigger? He thought 10X bigger! And the following exercise will teach you how to do the same, so that you can leave your limits behind and begin achieving the results that come from thinking 10X bigger.

Reflection Checkpoint

1. **First, take out a sheet of paper or notepad, and write down your biggest goal for your business this year.**

   Make it a specific and measurable goal so you can clearly know whether you have achieved it or not.

For example, "I want to be financially free," is not a specific or measurable goal. "I want to make $10,000 a month in passive income by December 31ˢᵗ this year," is a specific and measurable goal. Go ahead and write down that goal.

2. **Now multiply that goal by 10X.**

So if the goal is to make $10K, increase it to $100K.

If the goal is to make $100K, increase it to $1 Million.

If your goal is to make $1 Million, increase it to $10 Million.

3. **Then ask yourself: "What needs to happen for me to reach this new 10X goal?"**

Take your time, use your imagination and creativity, and let your mind answer the question. The goal of this exercise is to start thinking bigger so you can push against the limits you've put on your mind.

Let me give you an example:

Currently, I own a mobile app company, and one key goal upon releasing our apps is to sign up users who could later become paying customers. For our productivity apps, the ratio is about 5% of users become paying customers. So, for every 100 users that sign up, about 5 become paying customers. And out of those 5 customers, only 20% stick around. So, you get 1 true customer for every 100 users that sign up.

So, if I want 1 new long-term loyal customer per day, then I need to sign up 100 users per day.

That's not too bad. I can do that by promoting it to my email list, running Google or Facebook Ads, also by having great App Store and Google Play store optimization.

And at $60 a year per customer, 1 long-term loyal customer a day will land me a cool $21,900 per year ($60 x 365 = $21,900).

Now let's 10X that.

So I start with:

1 customer per day = 100 users signed up per day.

And if I 10X that, I'll get:

10 customers per day = 1000 users signed up per day.

So now let's answer the question:

"What needs to happen for me to reach this new 10X goal?"

This will mean either:

1. Spending 10X more ads spend (and I don't want that).
2. Promoting it to a 10X bigger email list (which I don't have)
3. Increasing organic Appstore or Google Play optimization (but there is a limit on what I can do here).

Or I could use more leveraged ways to get a thousand users signed up per day like:

1. Contact influencers with large audiences who are part of my target market, and ask them to promote my app for a percentage of the profits.
2. Create strategic partnerships with other businesses that service my target market but don't compete with me, and cross-promote each other.
3. Leverage other people's email lists with 100K subscribers or more.
4. Write a best-selling book and create a following of millions of people.
5. Do public speaking gigs at mega influencer-driven events full of thousands of people from my target market.
6. Create affiliate relationships with some influential people and hire the most successful affiliates in the world.

You see: multiplying my goal by 10X forced me to think differently, and to go after more creative, leveraged, and powerful strategies to get the results I needed.

You would think I would've thought of these ideas from the beginning. Yet, because my goals were so small, I settled for the path of least resistance. My marketing strategy focused on the most common methods that would only lead to incremental results.

But once I went 10X, it forced my mind to come up with more creative and leveraged ways to get a 10X bigger result.

And the financial result is:

At \$60 a year for each long-term loyal customer x 10 customers a day (or 3650 customers per year) = \$219,000.

Not bad for a mobile app.

I can always increase that revenue number by doubling the price, increasing our conversion rates, or running special campaigns to boost sales during special seasons. If I do that for 10–20 apps, I can build a successful mobile app business that makes millions, which I could later sell for 10X as much.

The idea is that multiplying your goals by 10X will force your mind to expand and figure out how to make that new 10X goal possible. It helps you create a new strategy, with new priorities that can help you hit your 10X goal or come close to it.

Now, will you be able to reach all these 10X goals that you are setting? Maybe, maybe not. But you will get substantially higher returns going after 10X goals than if you think small and go after small goals.

In other words, if you shoot for the stars, you may hit the stars. But even if you don't reach the stars, at least you will land on the moon, which is not too shabby either.

> **Tip:** Just for fun, try multiplying your goals by 10X again (100X), and see what new ideas you can come up with. You'd be surprised at the

creative ideas that you'll think up that could help reach goals that big.

Work 10X Faster

For Arnold Schwarzenegger, it took him 12–24 months from the time he started seriously training to when he won his first championship. He started training in his teens, and by the time he was 18, he won his first championship, and a year later, won his first Mr. Universe title.

How did he do it so quickly?

Previously, in this book, we talked about Parkinson's Law, which states that the time you set to do something is the time it takes you to do that thing. The belief that a task will take a certain amount of time drives us to spend that exact amount of time to complete it. This is a common pattern, but one that we can use to our advantage. For example, what if we put a time limit on ourselves that is 10X less than the original time we set to do something?

Let's say you have a project that is due in two weeks. Then why not set to do it in two days? Or if you have a product launch that you want to do in three months, why not do it in three weeks?

By embracing a 10X less mindset, suddenly, your mind starts to think of different and creative ways of accomplishing that task within a shorter timeframe.

Reflection Checkpoint

1. **First, take out the same sheet of paper you wrote your biggest business goal, and now put a time limit on that goal.**

   Make the time limit specific and measurable so that you can clearly figure out if you have achieved it or not. For example: "I want to make $10,000 a month in passive income," is a specific goal, but not measurable, because it doesn't have a specific and measurable time limit. "I want to make $10,000 a month, by the end of the next three months," is both specific and measurable.

   So go ahead and write down that timed goal.

2. **Now reduce the time limit of that goal by 10X.**

   So if the time was 3 years, make it 3 months.
   If it was 3 months, make it 3 weeks.
   If it was 3 weeks, make it 3 days.

3. **Then ask yourself: "What needs to happen to reach this goal in 10X less time?"**

An example for me would be marketing the book you are reading right now. After its release, my goal is:

I want 10,000 people to buy this book, after its release, in the next 6 months.

Normally, to reach that goal, I would use a marketing plan that included:

1. Run Amazon marketing ads to promote it on Amazon.
2. Run Google and Facebook Ads.
3. Send it out to my email list with a discount for purchase.
4. Put it out to the social media groups I am part of.
5. Presell the book while writing it to gather some initial sales.

That's a decent plan to get to my goal.

But what if I reduce the time by 10X? So then my new goal would be:

I want to have 10,000 people buy this book, after its release, in the next 6 WEEKS.

Then I ask myself: "What needs to happen for me to reach this new goal in 10X less time?"

I can either:

Use my previous marketing strategy but just add more money to it (which I don't want to do), like:

1. Spend more money to run even more Amazon Ads to promote it on Amazon.
2. Spend more money to run even more Google and Facebook Ads.
3. Send an email out to 10X more people on my email list (which I don't have).

4. Put out a post to 10X more people on social media (which I don't have access to).

Instead, because of the radically shorter time limit, I would have to be daring and get creative and change a few things up to reach that goal in less time.

For example, here's a better strategy:

1. Send the books to the top gurus in my field and get their endorsement.
2. Send the book to famous celebrities who can promote the book for me.
3. Send a copy to 50–100 influencers who service my target market and barter with them to promote it to their audiences.
4. Sell copies to potential strategic partners who can give them to their customers as an add-on to their services.
5. Leverage other people's email lists of 100K or more and share the profits that come from the email promotion of the book.
6. Reach the top affiliate marketers in the world to promote my book for a split of the profits.
7. Write such a mind-blowing and valuable book that people cannot help but spread the word and make it go viral.

The new time limit forced me to devise a different strategy that would produce more large-scale results in a more rapid timeframe.

But why didn't I think about these ideas before?

Because I thought I had a lot more time, and so I opted for the path of least resistance and followed the more common playbook. Once

I drastically changed my time limit, I chose a far more radical and impactful approach.

Reducing the time limit by 10X blew the limitations of my mind and allowed me to consider other options I wouldn't have thought of before. There was no sense of urgency before, but now, the sense of urgency to do whatever it takes to accomplish my goal has also increased 10X. It put a fire in my belly to get those 10K copies in the hands of new customers in the next few weeks.

Recently, I found myself in another similar situation when I had to decide how much time I would allot to writing this book. I knew that, normally, to write a high-quality bestseller took months or even years to complete. But then I thought, "According to whom?"

It made me think about the previous kid's book that I wrote that turned into an international bestseller. It didn't take me 5 years to write it. As a matter of fact, it didn't even take 5 months, or 5 weeks. It took me 5 hours.

So, my first thought was that it would take a minimum of 24 weeks to write this business book. But then I used the 10X exercise above and decided that I wouldn't write it in 24 weeks, I would write in 24 days.

The result? I was early. I completed all my writing for this book within 15 days. This is Parkinson's Law at work.

Therefore, multiplying your goals by 10X, and reducing the time limit to achieving those goals by 10X, will transform your mind so that your ordinary results will turn into 100X results.

Conclusion

Our outcomes are a direct result of our mindset and our expectations.

If you think small, you will get small outcomes. But if you multiply your goals by 10X and think big, you will exceed the limits on your mind. This will open you up to doing what it takes to receive abundant results.

Also, by working 10X quicker and setting radically reduced time limits on yourself, you will do things you never thought you could do and see results you never thought you would see, much faster and much greater than you ever thought possible.

So, increase your goals by 10X, and reduce your time by 10X. You will blow the limits off your mind that are holding you back, and you'll be able to get the 100X results you need to succeed.

Now, if you're like me, you may have started to freak out after previewing this 100X mindset, and considering the outrageous steps you would have to take to achieve these goals. It's ok, that's normal.

It's because you're starting to realize how much your character needs to catch up to your new 100X way of thinking. In other words, you will need to 100X your character if you want to produce 100X results.

So, if you are ready to build this 100X kind of character, then turn the page, because that is the subject of our next chapter.

ACTION STEPS

Think 10X Bigger!

1. Take out a sheet of paper, or notepad, and write down your business goals.
2. Multiply each goal by 10X (if you're brave, multiply them by 100X).
3. Ask yourself: What needs to happen to reach this new goal? (write down the action steps).
4. Now if you had no fear and no obstacles in your way, which one of these action steps could you put into practice right now?

Work 10X Faster

1. For each goal on your previous list, write down a specific and reasonable amount of time you think it would take to achieve that goal.
2. Now reduce each time limit by 10X (if you're brave, reduce it by 100X).
3. Then ask yourself: What needs to happen to reach each of these goals in less time? (write down the action steps).
4. Now if you had no fear and no obstacles, which one of these action steps could you start putting into practice right now?

100X YOUR CHARACTER

"Talent is a gift, but character is a choice."

– John C. Maxwell

In 1992, a poor, humble family immigrated to the United States from Kyiv, Ukraine, to escape the chaos caused by the collapse of communism in the Eastern bloc. In search of a new life, 16-year-old Jan Koum, with his mother and grandmother, moved to Mountain View, California, hoping to find peace and safety in the arms of a new country.

But instead of finding safety, they faced many challenges that worsened over time. Jan's father was supposed to join them, but he chose not to come, abandoning his wife and son to face hardships on their own. A few years later, Jan's father died in Ukraine. In the US, they lived in poverty, relying on government assistance for housing and food stamps to survive. To supplement their income, Jan's mother made extra money working as a babysitter, while Jan worked as a janitor in a grocery store. Shortly after they arrived in the US, Jan's mother was diagnosed with cancer, which would take her life 8 years later.

Jan also struggled with a steep language barrier and adapting to a new school and social environment without knowing any English. Being immigrants without a community, they also lacked any support system to help them get through the hardships they faced. On top of this, Jan's mother's cancer diagnosis put an emotional and financial strain on their little family.

This kind of harsh upbringing and difficult environment is unfortunately common in our world and would normally hinder most people from advancing in life. Which made what happened next even harder to believe.

Jan took an interest in computers. He taught himself computer programming by borrowing books from the library, studying between high school and work, and late into the night. He would buy any used books he could find to learn more and excel as a computer programmer. He even joined an elite underground hacking group to learn as much as he could and improve his skills.

In as little as two years, he was proficient enough to get a job at Ernst & Young as a software security tester.

At Ernst & Young, he was assigned to audit Yahoo, where he met Brian Acton, an employee at Yahoo. The two hit it off, and later, Jan Koum got a job at Yahoo, where he and Acton would work for the next decade. Yet, feeling unfulfilled at their jobs, they eventually quit Yahoo, took a year off, and applied to work at Facebook while vacationing, but were both denied.

After getting an iPhone, and seeing the rising market in mobile apps, Koum decided he wanted to build a simple messaging app that would make texting with his friends a little easier. So he created a user-friendly messaging app with a higher level of privacy and which was restricted from any form of advertising. And, on February 24, 2009 (Koum's birthday), he incorporated his new company and WhatsApp was born.

Later in Feb 2014, Facebook bought WhatsApp for a total of 19 billion dollars, making Jan Koum, and his partner, Brian Acton, billionaires. Koum was added to the board of directors of the company that had refused to hire him years before.

Throwing Out the Head Trash

The kind of life Jan Koum experienced during his childhood would normally knock most people down and prevent them from ever achieving anything worthwhile in their lives. These experiences fill us with what Perry Marshall likes to call "head trash" that become the mountains of luggage that prevent our lives from ever really taking off.

The question is: why did Jan Koum's life turn out differently?

Because instead of giving into his head trash, he was determined to throw it out by learning, growing, and improving himself. He was determined to adapt until he overcame his circumstances and achieved the goals he had set for himself and his family.

It's the same pattern you see in many successful people who did not let their circumstances determine the direction of their lives— people like Anthony Robbins, Oprah Winfrey, JK Rowling, Serena Williams, Keanu Reeves, LeBron James, and many more.

Now, turning the spotlight on us, the question we need to ask ourselves is:

What is the head trash preventing you from achieving your desired goals?

What is the story you are telling yourself that is holding you back from taking action?

What heavy emotional trash bags are weighing you down and preventing you from passionately reaching your potential?

We all have head trash. And it comes in many forms. It can come in the form of limiting beliefs we tell ourselves about what we can or can't do. Or the scarcity mindset that makes us believe that there aren't enough opportunities out there, and even if there are, we don't have access to them.

Head trash can come in the form of negative feelings we get when we think about what we need to do to get to the next level in our business and life. Or it could come in the form of beating yourself up about expectations you put on yourself, and which you continuously fail to meet.

No matter what it is, the reality is that overcoming head trash (throwing the trash out) will be the biggest driver to get you to

100X and beyond. Because only when you become what you need to become, can you do what you need to do.

In other words, if you want to 100X your results, then you need to 100X your character.

Why? Your decisions drive your actions. If your mind is preoccupied by head trash like fear and worry, or doubts and uncertainties, your ability to make good business decisions will be hindered.

Another reason is that you won't be able to take the deliberate and consistent actions your business needs to succeed if you are being distracted by your head trash for hours, days, or weeks on end.

Or the heavy emotional weight of your head trash will make leading your business challenging and burdensome. Further making it more difficult to stay motivated during tough times or lag every business faces.

But once you overcome your head trash, it feels just like unloading giant stinky bags filled with trash. You feel lighter, you think more clearly, you feel better. And this will help you make better decisions, stay focused, motivated, and pushes you to take consistent and deliberate actions your business needs to succeed.

It's All About Cause and Effect

Think of it this way: life is all about cause and effect. Every effect in the world is driven by some cause. It is a universal principle you see in science, technology and in life.

So if you are only getting a 1X or 2X effect in your life and business, it's because you are doing the 1X or 2X causes that are creating them. But if you want to get a 100X effect in your life and business, then you need to do the 100X causes.

This is where the head trash comes in. You would think changing from doing 1X actions to doing 100X actions would be simple. And the truth is, it is. But if the path to change from doing the 1X actions to doing the 100X actions is littered with mountains of head trash, then it will prevent you from doing what you need to do, unless you throw that trash away. You'll end up missing out on the 100X results you want, and instead, you'll stay stuck where you are for a very long time.

This is why some people's path to success can seem so hard, while another person's path to success appears to be so smooth and simple. Because our head trash determines the decisions we make and, ultimately, whether the path we follow will be smooth, or if that path will be a minefield.

But the important question we need to ask ourselves is:

Which path are you on right now (is it smooth or rocky)?
And more importantly, which path do you want to follow?

It's Time to 100X Your Character

There is no greater 100X driver for your business than your character growth and change. Because the better you do, the better your business will do. Therefore the greatest priority you must have if you want to get 100X results is to grow your character by 100X.

Jan Koum overcame his head trash by learning, growing, and adapting to his circumstances. In the same way, it's time to prioritize learning, growing, and improving your character if you want to 100X your results.

So what is it going to take to grow your character to get the 100X results you are looking for?

It's going to take Transformation, Internalization, Saturation, and Implementation.

Transformation

> "Success depends more on the clarity of your mind, emotions, and beliefs than on your marketing or business education."
> **— Perry Marshall**

Emotional maturity is the ability to determine what you want to feel anytime and anywhere. It sounds good on paper, I know. But how does one actually master being emotionally mature?

It starts by practicing something I like to call: the Universal Emotional Mastery Formula. It's as simple as this:

Think → Feel → Do

In other words, what you think determines what you feel, and what you feel determines what you do. If you want to change what you feel, and ultimately what you do, then you need to become better at mastering your thoughts.

I want to give you two very powerful exercises to master your mind, so that you can learn how to master your emotions and finally throw out the head trash that is stinking up your life.

The Power of Focus

Focus is one of the greatest gifts we've been blessed with as humans. This is because of how much influence our focus has on what we believe and feel. You see: focus has some great benefits because whatever you focus on **expands**, becomes most **important to you**, and **transforms into your reality.**

For example, have you ever been around someone who, even though things are great in their life, they just focus on the negative which makes them miserable? Or, have you ever been around someone who has gone through some of the most difficult experiences in their life, but because they focus on the positive parts of their life, they are still happy despite it? That is the power of focus.

Since our focus is determined by the questions we ask, here are some very powerful questions to ask yourself, so when your head trash starts to stink, you can more easily throw it out:

1. Why is this situation the best thing that could have ever happened to me?

2. What opportunities does this situation open up for me?
3. How is this situation helping me become more of the person I want to become?
4. What other things are going well in my life, despite this situation?

Let's try it out now:

Reflection Checkpoint

1. **Think of a situation you are not satisfied with right now in your business or life.**

2. **Now ask yourself:**
   a. How unsatisfied am I with this situation on a scale of 1–10?
   b. Now answer the Focus questions:
      i.   Why is this situation the best thing that could have ever happened to me?
      ii. What opportunities does this situation open up for me?
      iii. How will this situation help me grow to become the person I want to become?
      iv. What other things are going well in my life, despite this situation?
   c. Now, how unsatisfied do I feel about this situation on a scale of 1–10?

Does your head trash stink less? Great!

Now, let's move on to the second exercise.

The 4 Truth Questions

Limiting beliefs are beliefs that aren't true, but when you choose to believe they are true, they become true for you.

The world we live in is full of abundant opportunities that are accessible to just about anyone, especially if you live in a first-world country. But if internally you believe there are barely enough opportunities in the world (aka: scarcity mindset)—then this limiting belief (head trash) will dilute your motivation. Here is a powerful exercise that will help invalidate this kind of limiting belief so that you have less internal resistance toward achieving your goals.

It works by putting your limiting beliefs to the test, asking and answering 4 simple "truth" questions:

1. Is that really true?
2. Why not? (list 4–5 reasons it's not true).
3. What is true?
4. Why is that true? (list 4–5 reasons why it's true).

That's it. Simple, but very powerful.

Let's try it now:

Reflection Checkpoint

1. **Think of a situation that you are not satisfied with in your business or life.**

2. **Now ask yourself:**
   a. How unsatisfied am I with this situation on a scale of 1–10?
   b. What is your biggest fear that you believe will happen from this situation?
   c. Now, ask and answer the 4 Truth questions:
      i.   Is that really true?
      ii. Why not? (list 4–5 reasons it's not true).
      iii. What is true?
      iv. Why is that true? (list 4–5 reasons why it's true).
   d. Now, how unsatisfied do you feel about this situation, on a scale of 1–10?

Do you feel better about the situation? Awesome!

This is one of the most powerful exercises I have used for years to remove the head trash that occasionally pops up in my life and prevents me from achieving my goals. Every time I use it, I quickly throw out the trash and get moving toward doing what needs to be done.

Internalization

> "In order to create a positive action, we must create a positive vision."
> **—Dalai Lama**

Internalization is when you help your mind become so comfortable with a belief that it becomes part of you. You become more comfortable doing the things that someone with that belief would do, and ultimately you reap the rewards of those actions.

It's like if you took a billionaire, took all his or her money away and dropped him or her in a city somewhere. What do you think will happen after a year? He or she would probably be a billionaire all over again or very close to it. Why? Because they are internally programmed to be billionaires, and will naturally do what a billionaire does, which is make billions.

Now, what if you could program yourself to have the mindset of a millionaire? What do you think would eventually begin to happen in your life? You will become more comfortable doing what a millionaire does, and, eventually, you will start to reap the rewards from those actions.

In other words, you will become who you internally believe yourself to be.

And there is no quicker method to change your internal beliefs about yourself than visualization. Visualizing who you want to become is one of the most effective ways to internalize a new belief system and change yourself from the inside out.

For example, when I first decided to be financially free, I thought it would take me at least three years to achieve the goal of financial freedom. So when I started building toward this goal, I would take 5 minutes every day to visualize myself being financially free and the life I would live. The good news was that, before I knew it, I was completely financially free. But instead of it taking three years to achieve my goal, I achieved it in 7 months.

Now, being the skeptic that I was, I decided to try it again, but this time, I spent 5 minutes daily visualizing myself earning 7 figures. Six months later, I was earning 7 figures.

Again the skeptic, I tried it again, but I wanted to earn 8 figures this time. So I spent 5 minutes a day visualizing myself earning 8 figures. Twelve months later, I thought it hadn't worked. Until, after doing my taxes and calculating all the money I made, I realized I had made 8 figures.

Take it from me, visualization works, and it is the fastest and quickest way to internalize living a lifestyle of 100X.

Reflection Checkpoint

Let's try this exercise right now:

1. Think about a big business goal you want to accomplish.
2. How confident are you on a scale of 1–10 that you will achieve this goal?
3. Close your eyes and imagine yourself having arrived at this goal.
4. Take 5 minutes to think about all the evidence, in vivid detail, to prove you have already made it, like:
   a. Look at your bank account and see all the zeros.
   b. Step off your private plane for an island vacation in Fiji.
   c. Access your dashboard and see the 10,000 users who've signed up that day.
   d. Have lunch with your hero and visualize them asking *you* for advice.

5. Now, how confident are you on a scale of 1–10 that you will accomplish this goal?

6. Do this every day for 5 minutes a day.

    a. Preferably in the morning, but you can do it while driving or before bed.

Saturation

> "Show me your friends and I'll show you your future."
>
> **– Mark Ambrose**

Saturation is surrounding yourself with people who are already where you want to be. The idea here is that by spending time with these people, you will start becoming like them.

If you want to be a multi-millionaire, you need to spend time with multi-millionaires. If you want to become a thought leader, then you need to be around thought leaders. If you want to get 100X results in your life, then you need to spend time with people who are getting 100X results.

If you were to take stock of the people you spend time with the most, are these people at the level you want to be? Because whoever you are spending time with is probably a good indication of the type of person you are.

The good news is that the quickest way to change who you are is to be selective about who you spend time with. If you want to become a wealthy, successful entrepreneur who changes the world in a massive way, then you need to find these people and spend time with them. By doing so, you will eventually become them.

There are three ways that combined will help 100X your character very quickly and upgrade your relationships.

First: find people who are **great examples** of what you want to become and set-up as many meetings with them as possible. I would suggest at least 10 meetings per month, or at least 2 meetings a week.

Second: find the **groups** that these people are part of and join them. Granted, some of these groups aren't cheap, but I guarantee that you will make 100X your investment back very quickly.

Third: **read** as many books, **listen** to as many audio recordings, and **watch** as many videos as you can of the people you want to become. I read an average of 2–4 books a week, watch tons of videos and listen to a lot of audio recordings and podcasts. Why? Because I want to saturate myself with the way these people think so I can learn to think like them and become like them.

And don't just hear what they say but make it a habit that every time you read, listen, or watch these people, you will make one decision and take one action. Write it down and act on it the same day. If you do this week after week, and month after month, before long, you will see a radical transformation in your character, and ultimately, your life.

Conclusion

We all face challenges. Whether challenges that the world throws at us, or internal challenges caused by our head trash.

The question is: are you going to let these things stop you from achieving your goals? Or will you make the decision, like Jan Koum, and many other very successful individuals, to learn, grow and be who you need to be to achieve your goals in a massive way?

Because if you want to get 100X results, then you will need to 100X your character.

So, if you are brave enough to take the challenge to radically grow your character, you can speed up the process by focusing on:

- **Transformation**: empty out your head trash.
- **Internalization**: visualize the person you want to become and make it your identity.
- **Saturation**: surround yourself with people who are already where you want to be.

The next step, implementation, is the subject of our next chapter, which entails focusing your life on doing the most important things, mirroring the person you want to become.

Because if you want to 100X your results, then you're going to have to 100X your focus.

ACTION STEPS

1. Transformation

a. Take out a notepad and list all the head trash and internal resistance you feel. Then use the 4 Truth questions to invalidate those limiting beliefs.

2. Internalization

a. Dedicate 5 minutes daily to visualizing the person you want to be, and vividly imagine the evidence that you are already there.

3. Saturation

a. Decide to set-up 1–2 appointments a week with people who are great examples of where you want to be in your journey. And do whatever it takes to join as many groups as you can full of these people.

100X YOUR FOCUS

"I am like a mosquito in a nudist camp;
I know what I want to do, but I don't know
where to begin."
– Stephen Bayne

In 1464, in the renowned Carrara quarries in Tuscany, Italy, a 19-foot-tall block of marble called "Il Gigante" was excavated to be used to build a statue of Hercules for the Florence Cathedral.

However, its first sculptor, abandoned the project, and a subsequent attempt by other sculptors also ended in failure. For approximately 25 years, the marble lay untouched, exposed to the elements, and developed imperfections, including a significant crack.

But then, a young, ambitious, 26-year-old artist saw potential in this challenging piece of marble. He convinced the overseers of the construction of the Florence Cathedral to allow him to sculpt their latest statue using "Il Gigante" as the source material. Given his youth and the marble's notorious history, it was no small feat. Yet, his confidence and vision for the marble block was extraordinary, and his determination to sculpt from it convinced the overseers to give him the commission.

The artist's name was Michelangelo di Lodovico Buonarroti Simoni, and his project was the statue of David.

Michelangelo's approach to sculpting David from "Il Gigante" was revolutionary. He believed that the sculptor's role was not to create but to reveal the forms already present in the stone. Michelangelo saw his task as shaving away the marble and freeing the figure trapped within. He meticulously worked on the block, removing bits at a time, and transforming its flaws into features of one of the most celebrated sculptures in history.

Ultimately, the process Michelangelo used to sculpt David gave rise to his famous quote: "I saw the angel in the marble and carved until I set him free." This quote encapsulates his approach: an artist's role is to keep removing what is not wanted to uncover and free the inherent beauty hidden within the material.

Diamond in the Rough

Michelangelo's artistic approach is a perfect example of what the life of an entrepreneur is ultimately like. We start with a gigantic marble statue, and we must cut away at it, removing what is not important, to find the beautiful sculpture inside.

Our source material can be the thousands of tasks pulling on us every day in our business. Or it can also be the bustling marketplace with hundreds of competitors constantly trying to lure away our customers and prospects. Or making ourselves stand out from the tens of thousands of messages that customers are bombarded with every day.

No matter how you cut it, we have a daunting task ahead of us—identifying what is important amidst the mountain of customer needs, various tasks, competitors, and overwhelming messages surrounding us.

You may have experienced this when you felt overwhelmed with your ever-growing Todo list. Or you may have felt it when you were bombarded with all the daily choices you had to make, such as which vendors to choose, who to hire, which marketing tactic to try, and more.

And when the results don't pan out the way you wanted, then you must endure the frustration of trying it all over again.

The Power of Focus

What if you could find a way to quickly identify what is the most valuable, and set-up a routine to only do those things? Or what if, like Michelangelo, we can get into the routine of constantly shaving away all that is unnecessary in our business, so that only what is valuable remains?

There is a word that encapsulates the essence of both efforts, and that word is focus.

Focus is the ability to devote all your resources to achieving the most important thing in whatever you are doing. The ability to focus your time, effort, energy, and resources on one specific area doesn't just give you a big impact—the impact is multiplied exponentially.

Consider the example of a lightbulb and a laser. If you were to take power that you would normally use in a lightbulb—for example, a 60-watt power source—and use that as a power source for a laser, the laser could be quite powerful because lasers use energy more efficiently to produce light. Even though the same amount of energy is used for both, the laser is more powerful because it's more focused.

In the same way, when you focus, you can produce more power and impact in your business—which is especially important when you want to get an edge in the marketplace. Also, since we have limited time, effort, resources and money (TERM), the ability to focus becomes even more important. We only get a few shots before we run out of our limited resources, so you must make sure that every shot counts.

As a matter of fact, when Bill Gates' father gathered a group of men, including Warren Buffett, and asked them to share the one word that accounted for their success, both Gates and Buffett responded with the same word: Focus.

100X Your Focus

The key is to focus all your efforts only on the things that will bring you 10X more value, while using 10X less TERM to do it. And by doing this, your focus will produce 100X results.

In other words, if you want to 100X your results, then you will need to 100X your focus.

Here are two simple but powerful ways to 100X your focus and bring you the 100X results that you are looking for.

Identify What is Valuable

Identifying what to focus on can be very challenging considering the number of tasks required to make a business work. It's necessary to create a filter that will help us quickly identify valuable tasks, so that we can focus only on mastering them. Because **whatever gets measured gets mastered.**

The first thing we need to do is define what is considered "valuable," in a business. Business is designed to provide value based on how much profit, equity, and growth it provides. Therefore, those are great criteria to use to determine value.

So, value in business is determined by:

1. Revenue and profit that an activity generates.
2. Equity (internal value) that an activity creates.
3. Growth an activity helps the business achieve.

For example, let's consider bookkeeping. What would we find if we were to do an assessment of the value of bookkeeping using these criteria?

1. The revenue or profit the bookkeeping function generates: $0.
2. The equity that bookkeeping creates in the business: $0.
3. The growth the business achieves because of bookkeeping: In itself, it helps only maintain things and keep them exactly where they are. So the answer is zero.

Therefore, according to our criteria, even though bookkeeping is necessary, it's not valuable.

I know that right now many of you (especially the analytics) are crawling in your skin. But the reality is, unless it's bringing in money, equity, or propels your business to the next level of growth, it is not valuable.

Is it necessary? The answer is yes, which means that it needs to be done. But if it doesn't create value, then it cannot be done by the most valuable person in the business—who is you, the business owner.

Now let's consider something else, such as creating a joint venture (JV) partnership with a high-value referral partner. (A high-value referral partner is someone who already brings you business, but in a JV relationship, they will exclusively work with you, and bring you even more business.)

So let's ask the questions again:

1. How much profit does a high-value JV generate? $10K, $100K, $1M, and maybe more.
2. How much equity does high-value JV build in the business? A tremendous amount. Establishing a contractually exclusive relationship that will bring you more and more business for years to come substantially increases the equity value of your business, especially when you are ready to sell.
3. How much does it help you grow your business? If your vision includes multiplying your business value, then it will propel you to the next level very quickly.

A strategic joint venture partnership is extremely valuable and therefore, merits your undivided attention.

Reflection Checkpoint

Here is an exercise you can use to assess whether you are spending your TERM on things that produce value:

1. Make a list of everything you did the previous day for your business.
2. How much revenue, profit or equity did you create for your business from your efforts (put a dollar figure to each activity)?
3. Now, if you worked every day doing these same things for a year, how much value would you have created for your business?

Pretty revealing, isn't it?

If you want to focus on getting 100X more value from your efforts, then it will mean putting a dollar figure on everything you do. Then you need to dedicate your TERM to only doing the things that bring the most value. And by doing this, you'll make sure that every action you take guarantees that you are generating a high ROI for every task.

Identify What is Not Valuable and Stop Doing It

Like Michelangelo shaved off the marble until he found David, in the same way, if you want to 100X your results, you will need to shave off everything in your business that doesn't bring any value, leaving you only the tasks that are diamonds.

The truth is that 90% of the things in your business don't bring value. But many of them are very necessary. If you don't do them, they will cost you down the line.

For example, filing and paying your taxes doesn't bring any monetary, equity or growth value to your business. But if you don't do it, you'll be in a lot of trouble.

The key is to make sure these necessary items are done, but not by the most valuable person in the organization, who is you. So then, how do you make sure that the necessary items are completed, but not by you, so that you can focus on the highest value tasks in the business?

You need to Eliminate, Automate, Delegate, and Simplify (EADS).

Elimination
The first rule of focus is understanding that it is more valuable to eliminate tasks than it is to delegate them. This is because if the task can be eliminated, it creates less work for you and your organization as a whole and makes your organization even more efficient, effective, and productive.

The first thing you need to ask yourself when considering off-loading a task is:

How can I eliminate this task altogether?
You will find that many tasks are just things that we do because we are accustomed to doing them, and not because they bring any

value. By asking this question, you are forcing yourself to judge the value of the task, and then determine if the task is worth anyone's time and attention in your organization.

Also, this question triggers your mind to find creative ways to get the desired outcome without doing the task at all. For example, as a business consultant, one of the biggest lessons I learned was that 80% of what people do in business is a waste of time and can be eliminated. Things like, checking emails and texts 50 times a day, having frequent unnecessary meetings, or going after the wrong customers were common things that took up a lot of time but brought very little value.

When I finally started a business, I eliminated those tasks and many other non-value tasks altogether, and because of it, I became very successful at working 80% less than everyone else. This is how I was able to run one of my businesses working 15 minutes a day, and my second business, 15 minutes a month.

When off-loading tasks, the key is to eliminate first.

Automation
The definition of automation is simply getting the highest quality result without depending on any person (especially you). Now, you might be thinking that it's not possible to get a high-quality result this way because "if you need something done well, you have to do it yourself!" Or you may think that to make sure it is high-quality, a human being needs to oversee it.

The truth is that many productive people have effectively run very large organizations by automating all organization's processes. The key is to leverage systems and technology to do repetitive work for you so you can focus on the most important tasks and get the consistent results you need.

Technology provides a consistent high-quality result by using algorithms and artificial intelligence to continuously create the desired result while limiting human error. Systems also provide a consistent result because they provide humans with the guardrails necessary to maintain consistent effort and produce massive results.

Some examples of inexpensive automation systems include:

1. Using a customer relationship management (CRM) system like Salesforce.
2. Using a centralized project management software like Slack.
3. Recruiting top outsourced talent from Upwork.
4. Using financial automation software like QuickBooks.
5. Applying a suite of artificial intelligence (AI) software.

So when off-loading tasks, if you cannot eliminate a task, the automation question you need to ask yourself is:

"What technology has someone already built that I can use to automate this task?"

Delegation

If you cannot eliminate or automate, then delegation is the next step. To guarantee a great outcome (because people do make mistakes), here is an effective hierarchy list of who to delegate to.

You can use it to give you the best chance of getting the outcome you want:

1. **Experts and professionals**: Delegating (or outsourcing) to professionals and experts gives you the best chance of getting your desired outcome. They do the work 24/7 and have the day-to-day experience that others do not have. Also they can provide insight into problems you didn't know you had, solutions you did not know were available, and opportunities you did not know existed.
2. **Insiders**: If you know people with inside information about a project or industry that is essential to completing a task or a project, then insiders can give you the edge you need.
3. **Your Experienced Team**: Your team will be the last option because ideally, the task should be completed outside your organization first to free up your team to do more important work. But, when there is no other option, look for experienced team members who can best fulfill the project, and give you your desired outcome.

So when off-loading tasks, if you cannot eliminate, or automate a task, the delegation question you need to ask yourself is:

> *"Who can I delegate this task to that has the talent and expertise to guarantee the outcome I need?"*

Simplification

Last, if you cannot eliminate, automate, or delegate a task, and you must still get it done, then the final option is to simplify the task to its simplest form so that it will take less time, effort, resources, and money (TERM) to accomplish.

You can simplify by finding ways to:

1. Accomplish the task with **fewer steps**.
2. **Repurpose** the task so that you can accomplish multiple goals with the same effort.
3. Do **small portions** of the task, a bit at a time, so that it doesn't take up too much time or effort at any given moment.

The simplification question is:

"How can I reduce the steps in this task, so I can get it done with the least amount of TERM?"

For example, in my book publishing company, I had to spend a lot of time and effort writing a book. Then, after, I would have to find out the hard way, that the public wasn't even interested in my book. So, I asked myself the simplification question, which inspired me to go online and do research to find a simpler answer.

I learned that I could just inexpensively create a cover, and pre-sell the cover just to see if the public was even interested in my book. If the pre-sales did well, only then would I write the book. If the pre-sales did not do well, I would cancel the listing and start again with a new idea.

Stop Doing List

Ultimately, to help you shave away low-value tasks over time, you need to create a Stop Doing List. Like a To Do List, your stop doing list helps you incrementally remove low-value tasks from your routine until you have no more low-value tasks left to do.

You will discover that many of your obstacles come from doing things you should not be doing. So the stop doing list allows you to eliminate these obstacles one at a time until they are completely gone—eventually making you more and more productive, helping to create more and more value every day.

Reflection Checkpoint

1. Take out a notepad and make a list of everything you know you need to stop doing.
2. Now add items to the list that are necessary and must be done, but that do not bring revenue, profit, equity, or growth value.
3. Next, eliminate, automate, delegate, or simplify each tasks so that they are eventually crossed out from your list.
4. Do this every day, eliminating a few at a time, until they are completely gone.

Conclusion

We only have a limited amount of TERM. What you spend your time doing will determine the amount of value you create and the results you get. If you focus on low-value tasks, you will create little value. But if you focus on the highest value tasks in your business, you will create 100X results.

The best way to identify what is valuable in your business is to put a dollar value on every task you're responsible for. The tasks that produce the highest value in terms of revenue, profit, equity, and growth are the ones you need to do. But if a task produces little value, then you need to stop doing them by either eliminating, automating, delegating, or simplifying these tasks.

Shaving these low-level tasks off your plate little-by-little will allow the 100X value to rise through the marble, and like Michelangelo, you will be able to produce a business masterpiece you can be proud of.

Since all businesses share many commonalities, it is not surprising that there is a common list of the most important tasks that carry the most value in a business. If you are interested in knowing what is on that list, just turn the page, because that is the subject of our next chapter.

ACTION STEPS

1. Take out a sheet of paper or notepad, and list all the tasks you do daily in your business.
2. Next, put a dollar amount next to each task to signify how much revenue, profit, or equity each task produces ($1K, $10K, $100K, $1M).
3. Decide to commit to only doing the items that have the highest value.
4. For everything else, go through each task and ask yourself: How can I eliminate, automate, delegate, or simplify this task?
5. Then, create a stop doing list and make it a daily ritual to eliminate, automate, delegate, or simplify those non-valuable tasks.

100X YOUR PRODUCTIVITY

"A man who dares to waste one hour of time
has not discovered the value of life."
– Charles Darwin

Take a moment to think about the most successful people in the world today.

You probably thought of people like Elon Musk, Jeff Bezos, Warren Buffett, Oprah Winfrey, Mark Zuckerberg, or the other 3000 billionaires in the world. Or maybe you thought of a famous athlete, celebrity, or political figure.

I just have a few questions for you:

1. How many hours does each of those people have in their day?
2. How many hours do you have in your day?
3. If we all have the same number of hours in our day, why do you think they get different results than you do?

The answer is that these successful people are 100X more productive.

Successful people commit themselves to only doing the things that bring 100X returns for each hour in their day.

You see, contrary to popular belief, there is no such thing as time management. There is only task management. You can't choose to create or eliminate time, but you can choose which tasks you will do during that time.

And the tasks you choose to do will either bring you a huge 100X return or no return at all.

100X Productivity

100X productivity is deliberately choosing to do activities that lead to 100X returns. Elon Musk, Jeff Bezos, Mark Zuckerberg, Oprah Winfrey and many more successful people choose to do only the tasks with the biggest return potential, and they continually reap big returns because of this.

In other words, if you want to get 100X returns, you need to do tasks that have the potential to bring those 100X returns.

Yet, as obvious as this is, entrepreneurs face certain challenges that prevent them from focusing on the highest value tasks in their business. These are:

1. Getting distracted by the overwhelming number of things we must do.

2. Doing things that come naturally to us—unfortunately those things, in some cases, are not always the most valuable.
3. Having a limited amount of time to do anything.

So how does an entrepreneur overcome these very huge obstacles to productivity?

The key is to limit yourself to ONLY doing the tasks that produce the highest value.

Everything else is eliminated, automated, delegated, or simplified (EADS).

The 20%, 4%, and 1% Rule

Now let's refer to the famous Pareto Principle we spoke about earlier in the book, also known as the 80/20 rule.

It says that in any group or organization, roughly 80% of the things you do bring 20% of the results, while 20% of the things you do leads to 80% of the results.

Input	Output
20%	80%
80%	20%

If you were to take it further, you would also find that while...

1. 80% of the things you do brings 20% of the results
2. 20% of the things you do brings 80% of the results

This also means that:

3. 4% of the things you do brings 64% of the results*
   a. *20% of 20% is 4%; and
   b. 80% of 80% is 64%

4. 1% of the things you do brings 50% of the results**.
   a. **20% of 20% of 20% is 1%; and
   b. 80% of 80% of 80% is approximately 50%

You can see this more clearly in the table below:

Task Level	Input	Output
A	1%	50%
B	4%	64%
C	20%	80%
D	80%	20%

Now when you calculate the return for each of these, you see more clearly why focusing on high-value tasks have the potential to bring the greatest returns.

Task Level	Input	Output	Return
A	1%	50%	5000%
B	4%	64%	1600%
C	20%	80%	400%
D	80%	20%	25%

According to our table, we see that:

1. 80% D tasks will bring you a 25% return for your efforts,
2. 20% C tasks will bring you a 400% return,
3. 4% B tasks will bring you a 1600% return, and
4. 1% A tasks will bring you a whopping 5000% return for your efforts!

That is a powerful return!

And if we compare the impact of each group of tasks to each other, we find:

Task Level	Input	Output	Return	Impact
A	1%	50%	5000%	200X
B	4%	64%	1600%	64X
C	20%	80%	400%	16X
D	80%	20%	25%	1X

If you compare the difference in impact from a D-level task (80%) to an A-Level task (1%), the A-level tasks have a 200X greater impact compared to the D-Level low-value tasks!

Now, imagine if you were to consistently accomplish A-level, high-value tasks for the next 30 days. Where do you think your business will be?

Your business would get 200X great returns, than if you just spent your time doing the mountain of low-value tasks that clamor for our daily attention.

I learned most of the concepts in this chapter from my old mentor, David Finkel of Maui Mastermind. The one idea that he taught me—and that has stuck with me most—was the concept of the magic 1% that brings 50% of the results. It is by far the greatest thing that has allowed me to create a 100X Lifestyle for myself.

After learning this, I determined I would ONLY do the 1% that brought 50% of results. The more and more I strove to hit that 1%, the more value I began to create, and the more I began freeing up time for myself. Because of this, I became financially free at age 41, working only 5–10 hours a month, and building two 8-figure businesses. My goal in the next few years is to reach the 9 or 10 figure mark, but still only working 5–10 hours a month.

The Magic 1%

The good news is the list of tasks that bring the greatest value to your business is not long. I refer to this list as The Magic 1% because these tasks bring the highest value to every business. Therefore, these are the tasks that you, as the most valuable person in the business, needs to focus on. They are:**Finding Lucrative Business Ideas**: Find lucrative ideas and products that create massive value.

1. **Establishing Competitive Advantages**: Continually improve your competitive advantage.
2. **Exponential Marketing**: Identify and utilize exponential and explosive marketing opportunities.
3. **Creating Irresistible Sales Offers**: Create overwhelming value and reducing risk so that it makes your offers irresistible to the right customers.

4. **Designing Highly Efficient Systems**: Create lucrative and efficient systems that generate consistent value.

5. **Training a High-Value Team:** Recruit and develop high-powered team members and create high-powered teams.

6. **Establish a High-Value Network:** Build relationships and partnerships with high-value people and organizations (i.e.: referral relationships, high-value customers, joint ventures, centers of influence, funding sources, strategic partnerships, etc.)

7. **Leveraging Finance:** Obtain and effectively leverage large financial resources.

8. **Attracting Explosive Opportunities:** Identify and take advantage of valuable opportunities that can 100X your value and returns.

If you are not involved in doing the things on this list daily, then you will not create value for your business. But if these tasks are part of your daily routine, then you will create 100X, even 200X, greater impact and results.

These are so important that we will devote the entire third section of this book to practical ways of creating 100X results from them.

Create a Routine of High-Value Tasks

If you schedule it, it will be done. So you need to set your schedule in a way that prioritizes the 100X tasks that bring 100X returns.

Here's an exercise on how to do this:

Reflection Checkpoint

1. First, on your daily to-do list, make the first three items you do every day only tasks that come from the Magic 1% list.
2. Then, draw a line under those three things and write everything else you need to get done below it.
3. Your goal is not to do anything below the line, until everything above the line is accomplished.

This is called, "Living above the line."

Operating this way daily will force you to do high-value tasks first and create a successful routine that will bring consistent exponential 100X results.

Conclusion

The one big difference between successful people and unsuccessful people is what they do with the 24 hours in their day.

The good news is that we can choose to change tasks from things that bring $0, and start doing tasks that bring $10K, $100k and $1M to our pockets.

Therefore focus daily on ONLY doing the tasks that bring the greatest value in terms of revenue, equity, and growing your business. By doing this, it will only be a matter of time until you begin to reap the rewards of living a lifestyle of 100X (even 200X) productivity.

ACTION STEPS

1. Review the list of Magic 1% tasks in this chapter and schedule an hour every day to work on at least one of these tasks.
2. Before you engage in anything else in your day, commit to working on 3 of your Magic 1% tasks first.

100X YOUR STRATEGY

"In the midst of chaos, there is also opportunity."

– Sun Tzu

Sarah Blakely graduated from Florida State University in 1993 with ambitions to become a lawyer. She studied hard for the LSAT, but after taking the test, was informed that her scores were too low to enter law school. She studied even harder for the next six months and took the test again. Her scores were again too low, preventing her from starting her law career. Frustrated, she gave up on her dreams of becoming a lawyer and took any job she could find.

She managed to secure a job working as a greeter for the rides at Disney World. Later, she upgraded her job prospects by becoming a door-to-door fax machine salesperson. During her sales job, Blakely faced constant rejection and the physical discomfort of going door-to-door in the hot Florida weather.

One day, when Blakely was preparing for a party, she wanted to wear cream-colored pants and achieve a smooth look without showing her panty lines. Blakely faced a dilemma with her undergarments. She was considering using pantyhose, but they had seamed toes that didn't look right with open-toed shoes. But, she liked the way the pantyhose eliminated panty lines and made her body appear firmer. So, she cut the feet off a pair of control-top pantyhose and wore them under her pants.

Realizing that other women faced such a common problem, she came up with the idea to create a product that could provide the control and smoothness of pantyhose without the foot portion, so it could be worn with open-toed shoes. And without any experience in the fashion industry or as an entrepreneur, she took her life savings of $5000 and began designing a prototype.

Blakely persisted despite initial rejections and skepticism. She finally found a hosiery factory willing to produce her prototype after personally visiting many manufacturers. Then, after securing a patent for her new design, her new product, Spanx, was born.

She marketed her product online using social media and through posting humorous videos on YouTube. In the beginning, she had incremental success, but then she decided to shift her strategy toward getting into department stores.

In 2000, Blakely pitched her idea to various department stores and faced multiple rejections, but she persevered. Finally, she secured a meeting with Neiman Marcus, a luxury department store chain, which agreed to carry Spanx in seven stores.

Her big breakthrough came when Oprah Winfrey endorsed Spanx as one of her favorite products in 2000. This endorsement catapulted Spanx into the public eye and sales exploded. Spanx was a global brand by 2012.

Spanx's success transformed Blakely from her humble roots as a door-to-door fax machine salesperson to being the world's youngest self-made female billionaire by Forbes in 2012. This achievement was particularly noteworthy because she kept 100% ownership of the company and never received outside investment.

It's Time to Change Your Strategy

You may have experienced the challenge of working hard in your business, but only seeing incremental results. It's a common but frustrating situation that I and many entrepreneurs find ourselves in. What is most frustrating is that you know you have a great product or service, but you can't cut through all the noise to get it to your target market. Or you know you can do more and go far, but you just keep getting little results and don't know why.

Sarah Blakely faced a similar situation when she first tried to market her product. It was an amazing and useful product that millions of women would obviously benefit from, but her initial results were incremental at best.

Then her incremental results transformed into exponential and even explosive results, all because of one change.

She changed her strategy.

100X Your Strategy for Success

Blakely is a great example of how a different approach to success is needed if you want to go from getting incremental results to getting exponential or even explosive results. The truth is that incremental growth alone just won't cut it in a competitive landscape like entrepreneurship.

She shifted from the singular, incremental growth strategy that most entrepreneur's follow, to a creative 3-level approach to success. This 3-level approach is what I call the 100X Success Strategy.

The 100X Success Strategy is based on the idea that you can boost your results by 100X if you build your business not on one level, but on three levels. The three levels are:

1. Incremental Growth Level
2. Exponential Growth Level
3. Explosive Growth Level

This strategy combines the benefits that come from an incremental growth level, the big returns that come from the exponential growth level and the outrageous results created by the explosive growth level.

Let's look at these in more detail.

Incremental Growth Strategies

In the book *Atomic Habits*, James Clear mentions that a 1% increase in growth every day will produce a 3,700% increase over a year.

In other words: by making incremental gains, over time, you will get closer and closer to achieving a substantial level of success. Putting in daily incremental work to improve is the foundation of most success.

Sarah Blakely, at the beginning, kept learning, growing, and scaling her business bit by bit. She learned about fashion, manufacturing, and developing a quality product, while making small incremental improvements along the way. And because of her incremental efforts, her business began to pick up steam, and gain more customers over time. The results weren't mind-blowing, but she was making progress.

When it comes to business, most entrepreneurs restrict themselves to incremental growth strategies. They believe that if you do business right, it will grow linearly and incrementally over time, and hopefully, that will be enough to get all the success you need.

The challenge is that even after putting in a lot of effort, you end up only moving the needle a few percentages every year. A major reason for this is competition. Because of competition in the marketplace, you must put in massive effort just to get a little growth. And as this fierce competition continues to chip away at your small growth percentage, after a period of time, you begin to lose any growth you do make until there is no growth at all.

Another challenge is that inflation erodes the small growth you make because of the increasing costs of sustaining your business. Costs go up year after year, but because your growth doesn't go up in equal amounts, it severely limits your growth over time.

Last, what customers value today becomes tomorrow's expectation. So you need to keep improving and innovating to keep customers happy. Innovation costs money, and that eventually eats away at your small growth percentage until it wipes away any growth at all.

> **But what if: instead of growing by 1–2% per year, you grow 100%, 200% or even 1000% per year?**

Though it may be difficult to believe, this is exactly what Sarah Blakely did.

Exponential Growth Strategies

Exponential growth strategies rely on exponential triggers, that, when triggered, provide you with results of 10X–100X or more.

Sarah Blakely shifted from getting incremental results to getting exponential results by changing her marketing strategy. She went from only selling online to now focusing on establishing strategic partnerships with various department stores. By establishing a strategic partnership with Neiman Marcus, Spanx got increased publicity and credibility once they rolled out Spanx in their stores. This led to other future strategic partnerships with mass consumer brands like Target and help Spanx eventually achieve global distribution.

I experienced this in my children's publishing business. Though I was making consistent sales on Amazon, I was offered the opportunity to license the rights to sell our books to different publishing companies around the world, including Scholastic, the biggest children's publishing company in the world. This led to worldwide distribution in global markets that I would never have had access to. It was an exponential trigger that allowed me to exponentially multiply my results, and it cost me no upfront time, effort, resources or money (TERM) to do it.

The fact is that all businesses have exponential triggers that, when used, have a multiplying effect on your returns. These powerful tasks bring a level of impact that causes your business to jump to a 100X level very quickly.

In the previous chapter, we mentioned some of these tasks under the list of Magic 1% Tasks in business. The good news is that there are many more exponential triggers in business that will greatly magnify your returns if you devote the time to pursuing them.

Here is an additional list of exponential triggers that can multiply returns:

1. Find an **unmet customer need** in a high demand micro niche with low saturation.
2. **Negotiate an exclusive contract** with a vendor or manufacturer, which makes your product or service unique and more valuable in the marketplace.
3. Get an **endorsement** from a mega celebrity or influencer.
4. Create **an irresistible offer** for your customers.
5. Provide customers with **additional value that you can charge a premium for**, but where there is no or low cost for you to produce.
6. **Simplify your operations** to such a level that you can offer your products and services at a substantially lower price than

your competitors, and totally disrupt their business, capturing a large market share.

7. **Negotiate with your vendors** to add an additional feature that costs you almost nothing to provide, but which customers would happily pay a premium.

8. **Negotiate with a strategic partner** to distribute your product or service in larger markets, at no or low cost to you.

9. Turn your business into a **self-managed company** so that it multiplies your company's value when you are ready to sell.

If you don't just want to have incremental growth, then it's time to begin using exponential triggers in your business that can bring exponential results.

Explosive Growth Strategies

Explosive growth strategies are focused on taking advantage of special and rare opportunities that can 100X–1000X your returns and more.

When Oprah Winfrey mentioned Spanx on her "Oprah's favorite things" list in 2000, the publicity led to such a surge of demand for Spanx that the brand was never the same again. Oprah's influence and credibility created an explosion that brought millions of new customers to Spanx, as well as other endorsements from other influencers.

Now, since opportunities are usually random, explosive growth strategies are difficult to plan or predict. The question is: since explosive growth comes from random and unpredictable opportunities that are difficult to influence, how can we access them?

Well, opportunities are generally environment-dependent. Meaning that some environments attract more opportunities than others. Therefore you will increase your chances of finding and attracting these opportunities and achieving explosive growth by putting yourself in successful environments.

Examples of successful environments include:

1. Spending time with successful people.
2. Being part of business groups that are full of opportunities.
3. Tapping into a popular current trend.
4. Being part of a team of successful people.

We will discuss more on these in our chapter titled, 100X Your Opportunities.

You also need to set yourself up to be able to handle the explosive growth when it comes. Because when it does, your business will never be the same again.

For example, after Oprah's endorsement, Blakely could've been overwhelmed by the influx of millions of orders. But she had previously set her business up with the ability to quickly scale to meet the demand.

Using the 100X Success Strategy to 100X Your Results

I know what you are thinking: "It's hard enough to focus on one part of my business, and you want me to focus on three?"

I know how difficult it is to have a divided focus. Here's an effective mental model for using the 100X Success Strategy to 100X your results.

EADS the Incremental

Since the tasks that generate incremental growth are simple and repetitive, it is best to eliminate, automate, delegate, or simplify (EADS) the incremental growth areas of your business. For example, social media marketing is a simple and repetitive strategy that, though useful, generates incremental progress. Therefore, delegate this part of your marketing strategy to a social media marketing manager or agency. Or, if you have limited resources, you can use an automated social media marketing platform to minimize your time and effort.

Another example is answering customer queries and upselling customers who call into the call center. This is a necessary yet simple and repetitive process. This process can be automated by creating an AI chatbot that is trained to not only help, but to also upsell to customers so they can buy more products that will meet their needs. If the chatbot cannot answer some questions, they can also be routed to an outsourced customer service center.

Though incremental growth strategies do make up most of your business, you don't have to use your valuable time and effort in this area. You can EADS these tasks so that they can be taken care of by automation or someone else besides you.

Focus on Your Exponential Growth Strategies

Exponential growth strategies and exponential triggers create substantial value so they require your attention more than any other tasks in your business.

For example, an exponential trigger like recruiting a high-powered member for your team requires your valuable attention. This is because you need to make sure you can effectively evaluate if the team member is a good fit for your company. It also helps you make sure this team member can produce results, create synergy with your other team members and multiply results. If you delegate this to others, you may end up with a lower-quality member who brings your whole team down.

Another example is establishing strategic partnerships with high-value people and organizations. These kinds of partnerships can result in a massive boost to your sales and profits, and requires the expertise of the highest-value member of your team, which is you.

A good routine for activating exponential triggers in your business is to have 4–8 exponential triggers that you are working on implementing every month.

For example: in my publishing company, when I was first considering writing a children's book, I knew that competition for children's books was fierce. I needed to do something that would give me an exponential boost. Knowing that trends are a powerful exponential trigger, I researched the biggest trends for kids, which, at the time, was a video game named Minecraft. Then I designed all our first series of children's books as Minecraft fanfiction, and we ended up selling millions of copies when most authors have a challenge just selling their first thousand.

Position Yourself to Attract Explosive Opportunities

Explosive growth comes from opportunities, therefore, you need to devote time and effort to being in successful environments if you want to attract these opportunities. This includes meeting with at least 1–2 successful people a week. This also means being part of a group full of successful people and meeting with them at least 2–4 times a month.

Again, this is not an area you can delegate because the upside potential is so high that you must give it the best chance to succeed by giving it your special attention.

To best manage all three levels, here is a good rule of thumb:

1. Spend 80% of your time on exponential triggers and positioning yourself in successful environments that attract explosive opportunities.
2. Only spend 20% of your time on incremental strategies, focusing on making sure quality is being maintained and there is continued progress.

Conclusion

Most entrepreneurs want "Sarah Blakely level" type of business success. Unfortunately, the only progress that many entrepreneurs continue to achieve is incremental at best. But if you are tired of only getting incremental gains, then like Blakely, it's time to change your strategy.

In other words, if you want 100X results, then you need to 100X your strategy.

The 100X Success Strategy does this by pursuing success on three levels. The Incremental Growth level is necessary because it builds the foundation of your business. Yet, since most tasks on this level are simple and repetitive, it's best to eliminate, automate, delegate or simplify these tasks.

The Exponential Growth level is driven by exponential triggers that provide 100X greater results. Because of the value these tasks bring, they require most of your attention out of all the other tasks in the business.

The Explosive Growth Level is driven by opportunities that have the potential to bring mind blowing returns. Since, these opportunities are dependent on your environment, the best strategy is to position yourself in successful environments that attract these opportunities, including spending time with successful people or groups.

By applying the three levels of the 100X Success Strategy to your business, you'll be able to not only see incremental results but 100X your results in an exponential and explosive way.

Now that you've seen the kind of results that 100X Thinking can have on your life, it's now time, in Part 3 of this book, to see how to apply this way of thinking to your business so that you can also 100X your business results.

ACTION STEPS

1. Pull out a sheet of paper or notepad, make three columns and label them:
   a. Incremental
   b. Exponential
   c. Explosive
2. Think through the tasks you do in your business daily and put them in the column describing what kind of results it brings to your business.
   a. I.e.:
      i. Social media = incremental
      ii. Met with major distributor = exponential
      iii. Visited high level influencer conference = explosive
3. Eliminate, automate, delegate, or simplify all the items in the Incremental growth column.
4. Devote 80% of your time to doing the tasks in the Exponential and Explosive growth columns.

ARE YOU GETTING VALUE FROM THIS BOOK SO FAR?

If you are getting value from this book, then please help your other fellow entrepreneurs by leaving a review for this book.

Since a book is judged by its cover, they will need your help to know which books are a good read.

So if you feel like you've gotten a lot of value from this book so far, please let them know that they should read it too by giving your review.

★ ★ ★ ★ ★

Paperback
If you are reading the paperback, go to Amazon or wherever you bought this book, and leave a review right on the book's page.

eBook
If you are reading on Kindle or E-reader—scroll to the end of the book, and it will prompt a request for review for you.

Thanks again!

Now turn the page and get ready to have your business results multiplied by 100X!

PART 3

100X YOUR BUSINESS

100X YOUR BUSINESS IDEAS

"Don't find customers for your products, find products for your customers."
– Seth Godin

In 2011, two friends, Michael Dubin and Mark Levine were at a party and their conversation eventually steered toward the subject of razor blades. They complained about how expensive and overpriced razors were, and how inconvenient it was to buy them. Later on, they found out that some of their other friends had similar problems with their razors too.

Dubin and Levine decided to do some research and they noticed that the razor market was controlled by a few big brands with little competition, leading to high prices. They both saw an opportunity to challenge the status quo with a more affordable and convenient option.

They came up with a novel idea to provide good quality razors at a substantially cheaper price than the main competitors, and instead of selling them at retail stores, have them delivered on a subscription basis. The subscription-based model was still relatively new in the personal care industry at that time. Dubin and Levine recognized the potential of this idea: to offer great value to customers while also guaranteeing a steady revenue stream for themselves.

And with this idea, Dollar Shave Club was born.

Using an online, direct-to-consumer approach allowed Dollar Shave Club to cut out the middleman, reduce costs, and pass those savings onto the customers. Beyond just making a profit, they wanted to create value for consumers by providing a good-quality product at a significantly lower price, with a fun and unique brand experience. Their efforts paid off. Dollar Shave Club had over 3.2 million members by mid-2015—a testament to its growing popularity.

Unilever, a global giant in consumer goods, was looking to expand its footprint in the personal care market, particularly in the online space. Dollar Shave Club, with its strong brand presence, loyal customer base, and successful direct-to-consumer model, presented an ideal opportunity.

Unilever announced it would acquire Dollar Shave Club for $1 billion in cash in July 2016.

Not All Ideas are Created Equal

Dollar Shave Club is a great example of how to capitalize on a gap in the marketplace in such a way that it disrupts an entire market, which could ultimately end in a massive financial payday.

A gap is defined as when current providers aren't able to satisfy a customer's need. And if there are gaps in the marketplace, there will always be the potential to develop ideas that could solve these gaps in a way that will lead to massive financial returns.

But not all gaps are created equal. As an entrepreneur, I've experienced the situation where I try to fill a gap in the marketplace with a really great solution, but the idea falls flat. I've had many ideas, but for some reason, these ideas don't turn into huge disruptive technologies or large paydays. Mostly I just experience the exact opposite, where I've lost a lot of money just trying to get one person to buy my product.

Can you relate?

Why is it that so few ideas become huge successes while most ideas die in the marketplace? Or, even if we have initial success, our ideas eventually die out because we can't overcome the chasm in order to get it widely adopted by the masses?

We can write volumes on the subject, but in this book, we are most interested in how to get most of our products and services to succeed most of the time.

How do you do this?

If you don't want your ideas to fail but to produce substantial returns instead, then you will need to 100X your business ideas. And Dollar Shave Club (DSC) is one of the best examples of what it takes to create and drive ideas that generate 100X results and more.

This is because Dollar Shave Club fulfilled three very powerful principles, that, if you apply to your own business ideas, will multiply your results by 100X.

These are:

1. Create ideas that provide 10X more value than your competitors.
2. Deliver value to your customers using 10X less of your time, effort, resources, and money (TERM).
3. Fill a gap you believe in.

Provide 10X More Value Than Your Competitors

One of the biggest keys to getting your business ideas to produce exponential results is that you need to provide 10X greater value than your competitors.

If you only create a small percentage increase in value than your competitors, it will not motivate customers enough to endure the inconvenience of switching providers. Also, with only a small difference between you and your competitors, they will eventually copy you or add additional value to their own products, wiping away any edge that you had. But offering 10X greater value will give customers all the motivation they need to switch and spread the good news about your offering.

The easiest way to deliver 10X greater value for customers is to provide a product or service that is:

- **Priced 10X less** than the competition; or
- It's **10X easier to use** compared to the competition.

Offering a 10X Lower Price

It may sound radical to reduce your price by 10X, but the truth is that no matter how loyal customers are, they cannot resist an irresistible offer. This is especially true if customers felt that the items were overpriced to begin with.

Pricing an item 10X less will trigger their self-preservation gene, and they will relinquish any loyalty to any other provider. On the contrary, small percentage discounts, like 10–30%, though useful, don't provide a big enough incentive for customers to inconvenience themselves into switching.

But a 10X reduction in price will encourage customers to sacrifice their loyalties and substantially inconvenience themselves to get the offer.

Dollar Shave Club's initial offer to provide quality razors for $1 a month was so compelling that it motivated customers to drop their usual razor supplier (that they had for years) and sign up to be part of Dollar Shave Club's membership.

The low price point also made testing Dollar Shave Club an easy option, and once customers discovered the razors were of decent quality, they continued with the service. It was such an irresistible offer that Dollar Shave Club disrupted the major players in this market who hadn't been challenged for decades.

Our birdwatching binocular business also experienced a similar rapid capture of market share for the same reason. Our main competitor was charging an average of $1500–$2000 per binoculars. We decided to price our binoculars at 10X less their price ($150–$200), and we immediately began to capture a large share of the birdwatching binocular market. We provided above-average quality binoculars, at 1/10th of the price, which was just too much of an irresistible offer to ignore.

Making Things 10X Easier

Another method of providing 10X value includes making the product or service 10X easier to use than your competitors.

Customers crave great convenience above anything else including a great price. And the greater the convenience you can provide, the more customers are willing to change who they buy from—especially if you provide 10X more convenience.

The best example of this was the global transition from the Blackberry to the iPhone. Though Blackberry had 30% of the phone market in North America, their market share was quickly and significantly eaten away once the iPhone was released. The iPhone's touch screen, intuitive user interface, and the ecosystem it created with the Appstore made it so convenient to use that it took such a major chunk of market share from Blackberry that it never recovered.

Dollar Shave Club provided substantially greater convenience in purchasing their razors through their direct-to-consumer subscription model. Normally, to buy razors, a customer would have to travel to the retail store, and then find a clerk to unlock the cases the razors were stored in (yes, they were stored under lock and key during this time). Instead, through Dollar Shave Club's subscription model, razors could be automatically delivered to a customer's doorstep, month after month, without having to order every time.

This 10X greater convenience, combined with their 10X lower prices, was the one-two punch that knocked off a considerable amount of market share from their main competitors, and eventually landed them a billion-dollar payday.

If you want your business ideas to succeed in the marketplace, they need to provide 10X greater value to your customers by either providing 10X lower prices than your competitors or providing 10X greater convenience.

Here's an exercise to help you come up with ideas that can create 10X more value in your product or service:

Reflection Checkpoint

1. **Provide 10X greater value by decreasing price:**

   Ask yourself: How can I reduce my prices by 10X or close to it? (Write down 3–5 ideas).

   Ex: Here are a few solutions to help trigger some ideas:
   - Remove expensive features.
   - Convert to a digital format that costs less.
   - Reduce cost of delivery by using a simplified or digital delivery system.

2. **Provide 10X greater value by making it easier to use:**

Ask yourself: How can I make my product or service 10X easier to use than my competitor? (Write down 3–5 ideas).

Ex: Here are a few more solutions to help trigger some ideas.
- Create one-click solutions.
- Automate some tasks.
- Make integration seamless.

Provide Value to Customers Using 10X Less TERM

You're probably wondering how Dollar Shave Club was able to make a profit if their prices were 10X lower than their competitors. Or you're probably wondering if you did this, how you'll be able to operate with such small revenues. The fact is you will need to operate in a lean, efficient and streamlined way to provide this level of value and capture the market, as well as make great profits.

Earlier in the book, we spoke about the principle of Kaizen, and how there is always room for improvement and to operate in a way that reduces waste and cost.

Designing an operation that provides customers with value, constantly improves efficiency and reduces costs is the best way to gain substantial market share and maintain healthy profits.

Operating lean will also allow you to serve your customers more easily, scale your business, and continually reduce your costs—a benefit you can pass on to your customers. Further providing them with even greater value.

For example, from the beginning, Dollar Shave Club set-up their operations in a way that managed to keep their costs low and provide great value to their customers. Their operation included:

1. **Selling Directly Online:** They cut out the middleman by selling straight to customers over the internet.
2. **Recurring Payments Model:** Customers paid regularly through subscriptions, which led to the company enjoying a steady flow of income.
3. **Limited Product Selection:** Starting with just a few high-quality items, Dollar Shave Club kept things simple. Offering fewer products made it cheaper and less complex to produce.
4. **Smart Supply Chain:** They streamlined their operations by sourcing razors at competitive prices from top-notch suppliers.
5. **Slimmed-down Operations:** The company was all about lean management, keeping its running costs low. This included leveraging tech and automation to make operations smoother.
6. **Buzzworthy Marketing:** Their initial marketing video went viral, greatly enhancing their brand presence for little cost. Along with strong recommendations from happy customers, this buzz reduced the need to use expensive marketing efforts.
7. **Focusing on Customer Satisfaction:** Dollar Shave Club took customer care seriously. They used digital platforms to sell, engage with customers, gather feedback, and provide support.
8. **Making Decisions Based on Data:** The company constantly improved their products and processes by paying close attention to customers' pain points, feedback and how they

behaved. This data-driven strategy kept them in sync with what their customers wanted.

9. **Creating a Community**: Dollar Shave Club didn't just sell products but built a community. By making subscribers feel like they were part of something special, the company fostered loyalty, which was cheaper than trying to find new customers.

From my own experience in our binoculars business, we provided substantially lower prices to customers because we operated in such a lean way that it greatly reduced our costs. For example, we sold our products primarily on established marketplaces like Amazon, which both validated demand and gave us a large buying customer base. This greatly reduced our need to buy costly advertising or hire marketing companies. Since the buyers were already there, we didn't have to go out and find them. We didn't spend any money on advertising during the first two years of the business.

We also utilized Amazon fulfillment services that greatly lowered our time, effort, and cost. We asked suppliers to ship directly to Amazon, removing us completely from the equation. Our only job was mainly to order and pay for inventory. We outsourced the customer service aspect, which greatly reduced customer queries by preempting questions with online instruction tutorials and FAQs.

But by far the best decision we made to reduce costs was finding the best supplier who could create for us the highest quality product at our low price point. This substantially reduced customer issues, customer complaints and questions, and costs.

These efforts greatly reduced our time, effort, resources, and costs, so that we could operate leanly and pass off the cost savings to customers.

Therefore, if you want to increase the chances of your business idea succeeding, you need to provide customers with 10X the value in a way that uses 10X less time, effort, resources, and money (TERM) for you.

Here's an exercise to help you come up with ideas that can help provide value to customers using 10X less TERM:

Reflection Checkpoint

Provide Value for Customers Using 10X less TERM

1. **Ask:** How can I deliver value to my customers using 10X less TERM? (Write down 3–5 ideas)

   Ex: Here are a few solutions that can trigger some ideas:
   - Deliver value to your customer digitally instead of physically.
   - Automate your customer service with an AI chatbot. Like Dollar Shave Club, use a subscription model.
   - Form partnerships with other businesses to service your customers on your behalf.

Choose to Fill a Gap That is Important to You

This last piece of advice has been one of the most important principles in helping me create business ideas that have become highly successful.

You see: turning a business idea into a fully functioning enterprise takes a lot of blood, sweat and tears. Hopefully, the tips you're learning in this book will take a lot of the burden off your shoulders, and help you achieve success much faster and with less effort. But one thing that will motivate you through the tough times (and there will be many) is how meaningful the business gap you are trying to fill is to you.

Since you have the freedom to choose whatever gap you are going to fill—and there are many— why not choose a gap that is important to you?

More importantly, if you want to 100X your results, it's better to choose to fill a gap that has great meaning. This is because there aren't many things that multiply your results as much as the amount of passion you bring to the business you are trying to develop.

You will be more dedicated, passionate, creative, and hardworking if the gap you are trying to fill has an important purpose or value in your life. This will give you an edge in your business that cannot be copied and will result in outworking your competition, who might not have the same level of conviction as you do.

The more meaningful the venture, the more time and effort you will dedicate to being an expert at what you do. And, the greater expertise you have, the more effective and more strategic your decisions will be, leading to even greater results.

Also, the more meaningful the gap you choose to fill is for you, the more tenacity you will have to persist, persevere, and find creative and resourceful ways to overcome the challenging times every entrepreneur goes through to bring their ideas to market.

Obstacles are guaranteed to come, and if you don't really believe in what you are building, you will quickly give up when the going gets tough. But if your idea fulfills a strong purpose in your life, you will be more willing to fight through the obstacles until you arrive successfully at the other side.

Therefore, if you want to 100X your business idea and get 100X results, then choose to fill a gap in an area that is highly meaningful to you, so that you can unleash your passion, creativity, hard work, and expertise in a way that cannot be matched.

Conclusion

If you want your business ideas to succeed more often, you will need to make sure that your business ideas meets three very important criteria.First: you need to provide **10X greater value than your competitors** either by charging substantially lower prices or by making your solution substantially more convenient than your competitors'. Customers cannot resist an offer that provides considerably greater value than their competitors'. And next to price, there is nothing more important to customers than convenience. You will be able to grab immediate market share and even disrupt your main competitors if you provide vast greater value in either of these areas.

Second: to provide this value, you need to **run your operation in such a lean and cost-effective way** that you're able to deliver value to your customers with 10X less TERM. This not only makes it easier for you to service customers and scale, but it will provide substantial cost savings that you can pass to your customers, further creating even greater value.

So by providing customers with 10X more value, while using 10X less effort, you will create 100X greater returns for every business idea you bring to market.

Third: since you have the freedom to choose the gaps you want to fill, then **choose to fill a gap that is meaningful to you.** This will strengthen your resolve and give you the motivation to persevere when things get challenging.

Finding a great idea in a high-demand market is the beginning. Next, you need to make sure you can protect that idea by establishing a strong competitive advantage. If you want to learn how to add such a strong competitive advantage that will make it impossible for your competition to copy you, then turn the page, because that is the subject of our next chapter.

ACTION STEPS

1. Provide 10X Greater Value.
   a. Ask yourself:
      i. How can I reduce my prices by 10X or close to it?
      ii. How can I make my product or service 10X easier to use than my competitor's?

2. Provide Value for Customers Using 10X less TERM.
   a. Ask: How can I provide my customer value using 10X less TERM?
3. Choosing to Fill a Meaningful Gap.
   a. Ask: How meaningful is fulfilling this gap to me?

Pitfalls to Avoid

1. When choosing a gap to fill, make sure it's a big enough problem worth solving, and there are many customers willing to pay for it.
2. When testing your ideas, test passively, inexpensively, and risk free.
   a. The goal is to keep providing more value for customers while reducing your TERM.

100X YOUR COMPETITIVE ADVANTAGE

> "The most important thing to me is figuring out how big a moat there is around the business. What I love, of course, is a big castle and a big moat with piranhas and crocodiles."
> **– Warren Buffett**

Howard Schultz emerged from humble beginnings. Born in 1953 to a working-class family, Howard Schultz grew up in a low-income housing project in Brooklyn, New York. His early life in the Bayview Houses of Canarsie was marked by financial struggle, shaping his view of life through the challenges he faced.

Schultz was driven to succeed despite these early hardships. He excelled in sports, particularly football, which eventually led him to secure a football scholarship to Northern Michigan University.

This opportunity marked his first significant step away from the economic difficulties in his youth.

After graduating with a degree in Communications in 1975, Schultz entered the workforce, holding various jobs before eventually finding his way into the coffee business. He joined Starbucks, then a small Seattle-based coffee bean retailer.

Founded in 1971 by Jerry Baldwin, Zev Siegl, and Gordon Bowker, Starbucks initially focused on selling high-quality coffee beans and equipment. Schultz became their Director of Retail Operations and Marketing. A trip to Italy in 1983 was pivotal in transforming Schultz's vision of Starbucks. Schultz was inspired by the Italian coffee culture and envisioned Starbucks as a place where community and conversation were centered around premium coffee.

In 1985, Schultz's vision diverged from that of Starbucks' founders. He left to start his own coffeehouse chain named *Il Giornale*. This venture successfully replicated the Italian coffee bar experience. In 1987, Schultz's opportunity to reshape Starbucks came when he acquired the company with the help of investors. This acquisition marked the beginning of Starbucks' transformation into a global brand.

Schultz's leadership was characterized by a unique blend of innovative strategies and a strong focus on customer experience and employee satisfaction. He introduced espresso drinks and a cozy, inviting store ambiance, encouraging customers to linger. This 'Third Place' concept between home and work eventually became the hallmark of Starbucks.

Every Castle Needs a Moat

Under Schultz's leadership, Starbucks became more than a company that sold coffee. It became a symbol of culture and lifestyle—where people from all walks of life could gather.

What made Starbucks differentiate itself to such a level that it was able to outpace all its competitors and achieve global dominance?

It's an important question because entrepreneurs are facing greater and greater challenges in trying to differentiate themselves in the marketplace. With technology currently advancing at mind-numbing levels, becoming an entrepreneur has never been easier. Unfortunately, this lower barrier to entry has caused a tsunami of new entrepreneurs to enter the marketplace, resulting in a huge increase in competition.

Ultimately, this has created an environment where it is difficult to create a product or service that won't be quickly copied by someone else. And once your idea is copied, your solution becomes a commodity, leading to cheaper prices and lower profits for everyone.

You may have experienced this if you have been lucky enough to start your business and your sales began exploding from day one. Then suddenly, by year two or three, your sales and profits drop by half, and you have no idea what happened, or how to stop the bleeding. Normally, this rapid decrease in sales is caused by a competitor who found a way to copy your idea and is trying to undercut you on price.

Or you're trying to enter a market, but customers cannot differentiate between what you have to offer and what others are offering. So getting customers is almost impossible without spending a large amount of money on paid advertising, yet still getting little results.

Though it seems bleak, there is an answer to surviving and thriving in this fiercely competitive business environment. The answer is that your business will need to establish a strong competitive advantage.

Like a moat around a castle, a competitive advantage is when you add something to your product, service or business that prevents competitors from copying you and taking business from you. By keeping your offerings unique, the scarcity of your product greatly increases its value and ultimately, it increases the price people are willing to pay for it.

Iron-clad (Hard) Competitive Advantages

There are different types of competitive advantages or moats that you can add to your business. The main type is hard or "ironclad" competitive advantages. These are financial, contractual, or legal arrangements that offer substantial legal protections in case someone wants to copy you.

For example, here's a list of competitive advantages protected by law or through special agreements:

1. **Patents:** These give you an exclusive right to make, use, or sell your unique invention. It stops others from copying your idea for a certain amount of time.

2. **Trademarks:** These are special symbols, words, or logos that show your brand is unique. It stops others from using anything too similar.

3. **Exclusive Licenses:** This is an agreement where you get the special right to use, sell, or offer a product or technology that someone else created.

4. **Franchising Agreements:** This is a deal where you can use a well-known brand's name and way of doing business to open your own store or service.

5. **Long-term Supplier Contracts:** These are deals where you agree to buy products from a supplier for a long time at set prices, which helps you plan and budget better.

6. **Exclusive Distribution Rights:** This means you are the only one allowed to sell a particular product in a certain area or market.

7. **Government Contracts:** These are big, often long-term projects or services that you agree to provide exclusively to the government.

8. **Joint Ventures and Strategic Alliances:** This is when you team up with other businesses to combine strengths—like technology or access to new markets—to gain an advantage.

9. **Non-Compete Agreements:** Agreements with employees or business partners that prevent them from competing directly with your business for a certain period and within specific geographical areas.

10. **Intellectual Property Rights in Emerging Technologies:** This means owning the rights to new and advanced technologies, which can put you ahead in new and growing markets.

These advantages can give a business a big lead over others, and are very useful in building your brand and protecting your business from being copied by others.

For example, one of Howard Shultz's motivations in acquiring Starbucks was to take advantage of the already-established brand name and infrastructure. This gave him the strong competitive advantage and lead he needed to see his vision of a coffeehouse chain in every corner of the world come true.

For me, when I first went in the binoculars business, I discovered that selling binoculars was a highly competitive market. Therefore, from the beginning, I had to create some level of competitive advantage in the industry just to even get on the field. So I negotiated with our supplier to give us the exclusive right to sell a certain binocular product they already had in the marketplace. I was able to get them to agree to an exclusive contract right away since they hadn't had great success in selling that product. Then I used my marketing and sales skills to turn that product into a bestseller, and it has been one of the biggest money makers for our company.

Reflection Checkpoint

Take a minute and take inventory of your hard "iron-clad" competitive advantages:

1. How many hard (iron-clad) competitive advantages do I currently have in my business?
2. How can I add more?

Though these kinds of "hard" competitive advantages offer many benefits, they are sometimes difficult to come by. They may require a substantial investment, or may not be available at a particular time or place.

This is where dynamic (soft) competitive advantages come into play, which opens up opportunities to greatly multiply your competitive advantages, helping you 100X your results.

Dynamic (Soft) Competitive Advantages

Dynamic or Soft Competitive Advantages are advantages you can create on your own, but which still differentiate you from your competition and give you an edge in business.

Howard Shultz made Starbucks shine by using dynamic competitive advantages, which has become the hallmark of the Starbucks brand to this day.

For example, the success of Starbucks under Schultz is attributed to several key dynamic competitive advantages:

1. **Quality and Consistency Focus:** Schultz made sure Starbucks always used top-notch coffee beans and prepared their drinks in a consistent way. This meant customers could always expect a great and reliable coffee experience.
2. **Aggressive Expansion Plan:** Schultz led the charge in expanding Starbucks rapidly, both in the U.S. and internationally. Starbucks had grown to thousands of locations around the world by the early 2000s.
3. **The Starbucks Experience:** Schultz understood that Starbucks wasn't just selling coffee but was an entire experience. He designed the stores to be cozy and inviting, making people want to spend time there.
4. **Taking Care of Employees:** Schultz made sure Starbucks employees were treated well. He offered benefits like stock

options and health insurance to even part-time employees, creating a dedicated and happy workforce.

5. **Innovation and Adaptability:** Schultz kept Starbucks fresh and up-to-date by regularly introducing new products, embracing new technology, and adjusting to the latest market trends.

6. **Social Responsibility and Ethical Coffee Sourcing**: Schultz also focused on making sure Starbucks was socially responsible. He promoted the ethical sourcing of coffee beans, cared about the environment, and got involved in community projects.

These competitive advantages—all created internally by Starbucks themselves—greatly differentiated Starbucks from other chains and made them difficult to copy.

These advantages were a combination of adding external benefits customers valued and creating internal benefits that attracted great talent and made Starbucks a great employer. This combination made Starbucks into a powerhouse that was unmatched for years, and it was all built on a foundation of dynamic (soft) competitive advantages.

Therefore, if you don't have access to hard competitive advantages, then the solution is to create valuable dynamic ones of your own— either external dynamic competitive advantages your customers will value or internal dynamic competitive advantages that make your company a great place to work.

How to 100X Your Competitive Advantages

The best way to 100X your competitive advantages is to get involved in what I like to call Advantage Stacking. Advantage stacking is where you multiply the number of dynamic competitive advantages that you have so that it puts you further ahead of your competition, and it makes it very unlikely for them to be able to catch up.

The idea is similar to layering Kevlar. One layer of Kevlar won't stop a bullet. But stacking layers of Kevlar makes it possible to stop a round from a .44 Magnum.

Here are examples of 10 simple dynamic competitive advantages that you can begin to layer right now in your business, and can give you an edge over your competition:

1. **Brand**: Build a great brand that people wouldn't want to go anywhere else, even if the prices are cheaper somewhere else.
2. **Network effects**: Keep adding more and more people to your network, community, subscription, followers, etc., and give them so much value that they will love you and spread the word.
3. **Power Team**: Get some amazing and talented people to work exclusively for your team.
4. **Culture**: Create a highly effective, productive, and rewarding culture that produces great results and that your team loves to be part of.
5. **Leadership**: Be an outstanding leader who brings out the best in your people.
6. **Efficient System**: Optimize your system so that your lean operations can provide customers with substantial value using limited resources.
7. **Radically Reduce Costs**: Reduce your internal costs through technology, automation, and outsourcing, and give your customers reduced prices.

8. **Customer experience**: Provide a world-class customer experience and you'll easily separate yourself from the competition.
9. **Exclusive content**: Provide high-quality content your customers love that only you and your team can produce.
10. **Product or service quality**: Never stop increasing the quality of your products and services.

A big benefit of advantage stacking is that there is no limit to how many advantages you can add. Because of this, you can create so many advantages that your competition will have a difficult time keeping up with you. For example, you can stack 10, 20, 30 or even 100 advantages. It is unlikely that your competition is adding more than five competitive advantages. So the more you add, the quicker you'll outpace your competition.

Another benefit of advantage stacking is that many dynamic competitive advantages are character-based and require a lot of training and development. You cannot create these advantages overnight. Therefore, if you start building now, you will be able to blow past your competition a few years from now, and they won't have the time to catch up.

It's like that old saying that goes: The best time to start growing a tree is 20 years ago. By advantage stacking, your advantage tree will be fully grown before your competition even realizes they need to start planting.

This is the situation that many other coffee houses found themselves in when they tried to copy Starbucks. Starbucks had such a head start, and had mastered their dynamic competitive advantages so well, that competitors could not catch up, or even be in the same league.

The last great benefit of advantage stacking is that stacking your dynamic competitive advantages doesn't just create a linear advantage, but an exponential one. The more advantages you stack, the more they reinforce each other and create a synergy greater than each advantage alone. In other words, if you multiply your advantages, you will probably get 100X results or more.

For example, Starbucks created a transformational culture for their employees by: giving part-time employees insurance, excellent training, stock options, and great promotion opportunities. Ultimately, this resulted in such public goodwill that it multiplied their brand recognition 100-fold and their results as well.

Also, the concept of Starbucks as the "Third Place" was so ingrained in societies around the world that Starbucks was no longer known for its coffee but was renowned for being one of the best places to relax and meet people. People began to buy from Starbucks not for the coffee but for what Starbucks represented to them.

Conclusion

Because of the overwhelming amount of competition in the marketplace, you need to have strong competitive advantages to protect yourself from competition. If you have the opportunity, establishing iron-clad (hard) competitive advantages protected by contractual or legal means will give you an edge in the marketplace for a long time to come.

But if these iron-clad competitive advantages are not available to you, establishing dynamic (soft) competitive advantages is your next best option. Through advantage stacking, you can layer multiple dynamic competitive advantages on each other until you establish such a powerful position in the marketplace that, like Starbucks, your competition will be left in the dust.

Now that you've learned how to protect your business idea, you're ready to learn how to market your product or service to get 100X more customers than your competitors.

Hold onto your hat and turn the page to learn what it takes to 100X your marketing.

ACTION STEPS

1. Iron-clad (hard) Competitive Advantages
   a. Start establishing the easiest and least expensive iron-clad (hard) competitive advantages for your business first.
   b. Then go after establishing the more difficult contractual and legal competitive advantages as time goes on.

2. Dynamic (soft) Competitive Advantages
   a. Make a list of 10 or more dynamic competitive advantages you can begin establishing in your organization right away.
   b. Keep improving these dynamic advantages over time and adding more advantages as time goes on.

Pitfalls to Avoid

1. Don't just pick any dynamic advantages. Pick the dynamic advantages that are valuable to your customers. Survey your customers to identify what is important to them.
2. Also, pick the dynamic advantages that are valuable to your team. Survey your team to identify what is important to them and get their help in establishing these advantages.

100X YOUR MARKETING

"The aim of marketing is to make selling
superfluous."
– Peter Drucker

Like many entrepreneurs, Daymond John's journey to founding
FUBU started from humble beginnings. Born in 1969 in Brooklyn,
New York, Daymond John was raised in the Hollis neighborhood
of Queens.

Though John's entrepreneurial spirit, was evident from an early
age. He started a commuter van service and worked at Red Lobster
to fund his budding business. But it was the world of fashion that
captured his imagination and passion.

The idea for FUBU (For Us, By Us) was born in the early 1990s when
John noticed a gap in the market for woolen hats styled in the fash-
ion of those worn by hip-hop artists. Recognizing an opportunity,
John learned to sew these hats himself. With a modest budget of

$40, and using his mother's sewing machine, he created a collection of tie-top hats cheaper than those available in stores.

His mother taught him how to sew, a skill that would later become instrumental in his business endeavors. And wanting to inspire his entrepreneurial spirit, she mortgaged her house to provide seed money for FUBU, turning their home into a makeshift factory and office.

John's initial sales strategy was simple. He sold his hats on the streets of Queens, making $800 in a single day. This success was a clear indicator of the demand for his product. John and his partners, began sewing the FUBU logo on hockey jerseys, sweatshirts, and T-shirts to expand his market reach.

Later, John changed his marketing strategy by strategically loaning FUBU clothing to rappers for music video shoots. John was banking on the visibility and influence these artists had on their audience. This approach was cost-effective and gave the brand an air of coolness that resonated with the youth and the hip-hop community.

The breakthrough moment for FUBU came when John convinced LL Cool J, a childhood friend and hip-hop superstar, to wear a FUBU T-shirt in a 30-second promotional spot for The Gap. This ingenious move provided the brand with unparalleled exposure, as the ad aired nationally, introducing FUBU to a massive audience.

FUBU's growth exploded after this exposure. The brand expanded its product line and began to infiltrate major department stores across the United States. By the late 1990s, FUBU had positioned itself globally as a leading brand in the urban fashion market, with revenues reportedly reaching over $350 million annually, eventually earning a 6 billion dollar valuation at its peak.

It's Time for a New Strategy

John's story is one of determination and resourcefulness, but most of all, it demonstrates the power of utilizing different levels in marketing.

Though John's example is inspiring, it's not the common experience amongst most entrepreneurs when it comes to marketing their products or services. The most common experience is spending lots of time and money on marketing and only seeing incremental results. This slow drip of returns leads to either running out of money, motivation or both.

At best, most entrepreneurs only achieve incremental results in their marketing. But, with such small growth, competitors eventually increase their budgets making it easier for them to overtake any market share entrepreneur's get. Also, the cost of acquiring new customers becomes more expensive over time, resulting in any incremental gains being eroded.

It's not a pretty picture. I've experienced it. And I am sure you have experienced it also. The question is: why does this happen so often, and what can you do about it?

The biggest cause of this dilemma is that entrepreneurs normally only engage in marketing efforts at one level, leaving a substantial number of opportunities and money on the table. They tend to only market in a way that produces incremental results, and as we mentioned earlier, incremental results are not enough to survive in a fiercely competitive marketplace.

So how do you 100X your marketing results, instead of settling for incremental dwindling results?

Like Daymond John, the answer is that you need to 100X your marketing by attacking your marketing on multiple levels.

Reflection Checkpoint

1. Are you satisfied with the current results you are getting for your marketing? (Why, or why not?)
2. What marketing efforts are working well?
3. What marketing efforts are not working as well?
4. What do you think needs to change?

The 3 Levels of Marketing

To 100X your marketing results, you need to apply a multilevel approach to marketing. Similar to the 100X Success Strategy Sarah Blakely used, the 100X Marketing Strategy is broken up into incremental, exponential and explosive marketing efforts. Combined, these three levels will greatly multiply your business results like they did for Daymond John, Sarah Blakely and other successful entrepreneurs who applied this multilevel marketing strategy to their businesses.

Let's discuss each level in detail.

Level 1: Incremental Marketing (IM)

Incremental marketing includes marketing tactics that require consistent, incremental efforts to see results. These are marketing efforts you need to implement day-to-day, and they create incremental gains that grow over time when done consistently.

If used effectively, these marketing efforts provide a solid, steady growth of revenue over time. It's this predictability that allows incremental marketing to be the foundation of most marketing efforts and needs to make up 80% of your marketing strategy.

Examples of IM efforts include:

1. Content Marketing
2. Social media marketing
3. Email list building
4. SEO (Search Engine Optimization)
5. Referrals
6. Cold calling
7. Cold emailing
8. Networking
9. Workshops and webinars
10. Ads (Google and Facebook)

If you only focus on incremental marketing, you can expect slow progress and results for a long time. Usually, for many of these efforts, you won't expect to see results usually until after 12–24 months.

If the competition is fierce in your industry, you may have to wait three years or more to see results if you're lucky. Unfortunately, this means pouring out money month after month and not knowing if you will see a return. More commonly than not, most entrepreneurs run out of money or patience before they see the results they are looking for.

The other challenge with incremental marketing is that it doesn't produce much return at the beginning because the time and expense you use for these marketing efforts eats up all your profits. So you must go months without a profit, waiting and hoping for an exponential growth curve that might never come.

Though it seems bleak, there are successful strategies that can help you get the most out of incremental marketing efforts.

For example, Daymond John also experienced incremental growth when he first began selling his product. Like most businesses, growth was slow at the beginning. But instead of wasting money on marketing and advertising for results he wouldn't see for a long time, he and his partners kept costs down by going to the streets and selling directly to consumers.

We had a similar experience in our birdwatching binoculars business. We made the decision to spend absolutely no money on advertising for the first two years of our business because we didn't want to waste money that we weren't sure would bring a return. One of the best strategies was to first test our products on a marketplace like Amazon. On Amazon, we listed and marketed our product with no upfront fee. Also, Amazon had an entire buying community where we could test the demand for our product without spending any money on advertising.

Also, by listing our products on Amazon, if the product didn't achieve daily sales within 60 days, on its own without advertising, then we would find another product to sell. Our binocular product was the 6th product we tried that brought in daily sales a few days after we posted it without any advertising whatsoever.

We asked friends and family to provide reviews to give the product more credibility. Then we designed great pictures for our product listing, and created emotionally compelling sales copy, that we did in house, so it costed us nothing upfront. Eventually, on its own, and without spending additional money on marketing, the product began having daily sales, which continued to increase for 2 years. Later, we decided to add money to advertising to boost the results.

Therefore, one key to managing incremental marketing is to focus only on low-cost advertising efforts until you begin producing large results. Another key is to focus first on incremental marketing areas that bring short-term quick results. The initial return you get from these short-term efforts will not only help motivate you, but give you resources to put toward the longer-term marketing efforts as well.

Here is a simple stair-step plan to use when working with incremental marketing areas to minimize time and cost, but maximize your returns:

Stage 1: Focus on Short-term low-cost efforts (30–90 days).

1. Referrals
2. Cold calling
3. Cold emailing
4. Free Workshops and webinars

Stage 2: Start putting time and money into Mid-term efforts (3–12 months).

1. Networking
2. Social media marketing (posting)
3. Content marketing
4. Email marketing
5. Affiliate Marketing

Stage 3: Begin investing time and money in Long-term (12+ months) efforts, steadily increasing your investment as you see results.

1. SEO
2. Ads (Google and Facebook)

Level 2: Exponential Marketing (EM)

Exponential Marketing are marketing efforts that produce rapid, large-scale results with minimum effort. These are the hot 20% marketing efforts that usually 10X your normal returns. And because of this, they lead to the most 10X jumps in your business and can easily take your business to new heights.

For example, even though Daymond John initially started selling his product on the street to gain traction, he quickly shifted his strategy to going after marketing efforts that would produce exponential results. He did this by capitalizing on the hip hop culture that was brewing at the time. He lent his clothing to rappers and other music influencers to use in their music videos, hoping that his brand would gain rapid visibility to their large audiences. This strategy turned out to be a huge success because association with popular music artists gave FUBU credibility that resonated with its target market and catapulted it to a new level.

Exponential marketing is the special forces unit of your marketing efforts and should be used strategically. When used well, like in FUBU's case, it has the potential to take your entire organization to a whole new level. Like riding a current, exponential marketing creates massive momentum that quickly and effortlessly produces large-scale results, with very low cost and effort.

Here are some examples of exponential marketing tactics that can boost your marketing by 10X even 100X or more:

1. **Cross-sell or upsell** new products and services to your current customer base.
2. **Partner with influencers** with access to large audiences full of your target market.
3. **Partner with business or industry leaders** that cater to your target market, but don't compete with you.
4. **Group Marketing** by building influence in online groups, then promoting your products and services as a market leader.
5. Partner with highly effective **affiliate marketers**.

6. Sign up for **guest speaking engagements** on various platforms like live events, podcasts, video interviews, and blogs that can give you access to a very large audience of your target market.

7. Gain **referral partners** who have access to thousands of your target market.

8. Write a **best-selling book** that resonates with your target market, and quickly gives you authority and mass influence.

9. Gain **premium, front-page listing on Marketplaces** with valuable keywords (Amazon, App Store, etc.).

10. **Trend Content marketing** that discusses current hot trends in very high demand with low saturation.

Exponential marketing requires most of your attention since it has the biggest impact on your marketing that you can control. Therefore, the exponential marketing efforts above should take 80% of your marketing investment and focus.

Level 3: Explosive Marketing (XM)

Like its name, explosive marketing efforts tend to create such a game-changing and explosive impact on sales that the returns are in the realm of 100X and above. These are not like the special forces. They are the atomic bomb marketing efforts that impact everything.

Perhaps the most famous unexpected explosive marketing opportunity for Daymond John and FUBU came when LL Cool J, a childhood friend and a hip-hop superstar, was featured in a Gap commercial in 1997. Unbeknownst to Gap, LL Cool J subtly incorporated a FUBU hat and a T-shirt with "FB" (for FUBU) into his outfit. He even rapped "For Us, By Us, on the low," giving

FUBU national exposure on a major retailer's platform. This was a massive, unplanned boost for FUBU, capitalizing on The Gap's audience and marketing budget.

FUBU's international appeal was another unexpected opportunity for John. While John understood hip-hop culture's influence, the global demand for FUBU products was an unexpected but pleasant surprise. The brand resonated with consumers in various countries, leading to its quick, international expansion, and significantly boosting its success.

Though highly valuable, explosive marketing opportunities are difficult to time or plan. This is because, like most opportunities, they are random and unpredictable. The key is to put yourself in the right environment that attracts these opportunities so that you'll have a much higher chance of taking advantage of them.

Here are some environments or efforts that can lead to some explosive marketing opportunities:

1. **Routinely meeting with successful and influential people**
   a. Setting up weekly meetings with influential people will lead to opportunities and introductions to other influential people.
   b. Make sure you bring value to your relationships, which will speed up the process.

2. **Being part of groups led by or frequented by influencers**
   a. Many influencers have training groups, masterminds, or social networks where they spend most of their time. By

involving yourself in these groups, you will increase your chances of not only finding opportunities, but also being introduced to other influential people.

3. **Charitable celebrity galas and fundraisers**
   a. Being involved in charitable events thrown by mega celebrities or mega influencers usually leads to introductions that can lead to very large opportunities.

4. **Being an expert**
   a. Influential people look for experts. By positioning yourself as an expert, you will be sought after when they have a problem that needs solving.
   b. Proving your value by freely sharing your expertise with the world will give you a better chance of being seen as well.

5. **Write a book**
   a. Writing a best-selling book automatically gives you authority and expert status.

6. **Produce a phenomenal, world-class product or service**
   a. Influencers want the best products and services, and if your product or service is the best in its class, you can be sure an influencer will somehow use it.

Explosive marketing provides opportunities of a lifetime, which bring gains in the 100X, 1000X and even 10,000X level.

Prioritize positioning yourself in environments that will increase your chances of attracting explosive opportunities if you want to take advantage of them.

But be prepared when these opportunities come because when they do happen, they will come big and come fast. If you are ready, you will be able to experience the full 100X+ rewards as a result of explosive marketing.

The 100X Marketing Success Strategy

Daymond John realized his vision and created a brand worth billions of dollars by using the 3-Level approach to marketing. He:

- Used **grassroots marketing tactics**
- **Leveraged** the hip-hop movement
- Took **advantage of opportunities** that would catapult his brand to global statusIn the same way, you can multiply your marketing results by 100X by applying a 3-Level approach to your marketing that focuses on incremental, exponential, and explosive marketing efforts.

Here's a simple but powerful marketing strategy that utilizes the right amount of time and effort for each.

Incremental Marketing (IM):
- For IM, use low-cost, and short-term marketing tactics to get quick results.
- Since many IM efforts are repetitive and bring incremental results, only use 20% of your time and effort in this area.
- Automate, delegate, or simplify these IM efforts, to free you up to focus on the more impactful marketing areas.
- Only spend your time on IM efforts to check quality and to make sure that progress continues to increase.

Exponential Marketing (EM):

- Since exponential marketing efforts bring the biggest results you can control, you need to dedicate 80% of your time, effort, resources, and money (TERM) to these efforts.
- Grow your EM by making it a priority, and start building high-value relationships (strategic partners, influencers, industry leaders, etc.) to create agreements that multiply your returns.
- Bring high value to these influential relationships, and they will be happy to utilize their influence to provide you value as well.

Explosive Marketing:

- Explosive marketing opportunities are unpredictable. Therefore, position yourself in environments with the highest potential to attract such opportunities.
- Invest money to be part of groups full of influential individuals so you can leverage your time and meet many of them in a short period of time.
- Bring high value to these influential groups so that you can build a reputation.
- Produce a world-class product or service that leads to word-of-mouth credibility and authority.
- Be an expert in your field and freely give away your expertise to the public so that you can become well-known.

Conclusion

Entrepreneurs aren't cursed to only get incremental results for all their marketing efforts. You can supercharge your marketing efforts by using the 100X Marketing Strategy and attack your marketing on three levels. You can quickly 100X results by:

- Automating and delegating your incremental marketing.
- Devoting 80% of your time to exponential marketing.
- Putting yourself in environments that attract explosive marketing opportunities.

And like Daymond John, your results will become an inspiration for entrepreneurs everywhere for years to come.

Now that you've learned how to 100X your marketing results, just turn the page to the next chapter, so you can learn how to 100X your sales, by closing 90% of your sales prospects every time.

ACTION STEPS

1. Reduce your expenses and use low-cost strategies for your incremental marketing efforts.
2. Delegate, automate, or simplify your incremental marketing efforts, and only devote 20% of your focus to ensure quality and manage progress.
3. Dedicate 1–2 hours daily to implementing your exponential marketing tactics.
4. Schedule 2–4 sessions a month to be part of groups with influential people and bring them value.

Pitfalls to Avoid

1. Exponential marketing can be inconsistent, but don't let that stop your efforts.
2. Explosive marketing opportunities are random and unpredictable, so be patient with them.
3. Only check incremental marketing efforts once a week or once a month for quality and progress.

100X YOUR SALES

"Price becomes irrelevant when the customer clearly sees the value being offered."

- Tom Snyder

"My father came here with $1,000. He didn't speak English, but he had a medical degree," Alex Hormozi recounted in an interview. "My father said, 'They took everything we had, but they couldn't take my education.'"

Born as a first-generation Iranian-American, Alex Hormozi's early career was full of struggle to find his own path. He realized his career choices were more driven by his father's aspirations than his own.

Hormozi realized everything he did in his life was in pursuit of his father's approval, and that he had never really made decisions for himself or for his own joy. Ultimately, it became clear that he didn't want to live the life that he was living. So even at the risk of disappointing his father, he decided to set out on his own.

He made a bold decision to pursue his entrepreneurial dreams, starting with opening a gym business in Huntington Beach, California. He demonstrated his knack for growing and scaling businesses by successfully setting up six locations within three years.

The turning point in Hormozi's career came with his venture, Gym Launch, which he founded in 2016. Gym Launch was a culmination of his experiences and learnings from expanding his own gym business, which he packaged as a consulting service and sold to other gym owners. This model proved to be immensely successful, helping more than 4,500 facilities across 13 countries to grow and succeed. This licensing model became a pivotal strategy, showcasing his ability to effectively package and market his business knowledge.

Hormozi's sales techniques and business models centered around providing exceptional value to customers. His approach was characterized by creating irresistible offers and articulating the customer's pain points, which he encapsulated in his books, "Gym Launch Secrets" and "$100M Offers."

By 2021, Hormozi had scaled and exited seven companies, with his most notable exit being the majority sale of his licensing company for $46.2 million. This was a testament to his ability to build and scale diverse businesses, ranging from software to e-commerce.

Founded in 2020, Hormozi's latest venture, Acquisition.com, is a platform where he invests both his financial and intellectual capital in other businesses. His portfolio under Acquisition.com is valued at over $100 million, a testament to his success in identifying and nurturing high-potential ventures.

A Riddle Wrapped in a Mystery Inside an Enigma

"It is a riddle, wrapped in a mystery, inside
an enigma."
– Winston Churchill

Alex Hormozi is a great example of how increasing your sales ability has a monumental impact on multiplying your business success. As a matter of fact, some believe that your sales ability is the number one criterion to determine if you will make it in the world of entrepreneurship.

Unfortunately, the Winston Churchill quote above describes how entrepreneurs feel when they think about sales. They know it is necessary, they even know it is critical, but getting buyers in front of them to say yes eludes them, and the bottom line of their business suffers greatly because of it.

You may have had a similar experience. I know I have. See if you can relate to these:

- You design a beautiful landing page and pay to drive traffic to it, but it's just not converting.
- You set-up a lot of appointments, but you get little to no sales from them.
- You know you have a great product, but the public can't see what you see, and you scratch your head trying to figure out why.
- Or my favorite, you get in front of a prospect, you get through your sales pitch, you even give them a great discount offer, but, at the end, they say, "I'll think about it."

Then you go on the internet and hear people talk about how they've sold 100 million dollars' worth of products and services. Or you hear about a mobile app that is getting millions of downloads. Or you see videos of people getting millions of subscribers. And you just end up scratching your head thinking that this sales thing is a riddle, wrapped in a mystery, inside an enigma.

Value is in the Eye of the Beholder

The good news is that sales are a lot simpler than you think. So simple in fact that anyone can master it.

The most important thing to understand about sales is that the key that determines if you get a sale or not is found in one word.

And that word is Value.

Meaning, that if a person sees value in what you have to offer, they will buy it. But if they don't see value, they will not buy it. It's as simple as that.

And value is determined by either removing a person's pain by solving their problem or bringing a person pleasure. The better your product or service can do either of these, the more value it creates for the customer.

The good news is that if people are not buying what you are offering—though it might feel awful—it is a crystal-clear sign that they don't see the value, and you've got some work to do.

There are only two reasons why customers do not see value in what you have to offer. Either:

1. You're offering it to the wrong person.
2. You're not communicating enough value to justify the price you are asking for.

Finding Your Ideal Customer

Take a minute, grab a notepad and answer this question:

When you think of your ideal customer, who would that be?

The obvious answer will be the person who absolutely loves your product or service, and that it makes exceedingly happy. Not only that, but they are grateful to have it, can't live without it, talk about it with everyone, and start promoting it to others. And once you find this person, it is the beginning of a beautiful relationship that leads to exploding sales.

As obvious as this sounds, surprisingly, one of the biggest reasons entrepreneurs have such a difficult time selling their products or services is that they keep offering it to the wrong people.

A major reason for this is that entrepreneurs have a habit of believing that their product or service is a good fit for most people. So they cast a wide net, spending their hard-earned money (or borrowed) on paid advertising that brings little results. Or they get in front of appointment after appointment resulting in little to no sales.

Another reason entrepreneurs choose the wrong customers is that they try to sell their products and services to anyone with a pulse. And when they don't get the sale, they quickly find out that most of these prospects couldn't afford it in the first place.

A better strategy is to narrow your ideal customer criteria to only include your absolute die-hard superfans who see great value in what you have to offer, and also have lots of discretionary income. Then design your business to only sell to them.

For example, once I learned this one lesson, I went from closing 20–30% of the prospects I met with (sad I know) to closing over 90% of the prospects that I got in front of. As a matter of fact, I was able to close 90% of the entire room at one workshop.

What changed? I just decided that I would only get in front of potential customers who absolutely wanted what I was offering, respected how much value I was bringing them and who had plenty of money to pay for the service. Once I narrowed my meetings to those people, all my meetings ended in one word: "Yes!"

The best news is that once you have a crop of these superfans as your customers, they will turn into the salespeople you'll need to promote your products and services to others, resulting in even more sales.

Here's a list of some great sources for finding your crop of super-fans:

1. **Customer Referral Programs**: Encourage existing customers to refer friends who might be superfans. Offer incentives for successful referrals.

2. **Influencer Partnerships**: Partner with influencers who have a dedicated following in your niche. Leverage their audience to find potential superfans.

3. **YouTube Channels**: Collaborate with content creators who focus on your industry or niche. Engage with their audience in the comments section.

4. **Email Newsletters**: Build an email list and send out regular newsletters. Include exclusive content or early access to products to foster a sense of belonging.

5. **Content Creation:** Create valuable and shareable content that resonates with your target audience. Use blog posts, podcasts, or videos to attract and engage potential superfans.

6. **Social Media Platforms**: Engage with users on platforms like Instagram, LinkedIn, Twitter, Facebook, etc. Use hashtags and keywords to find conversations about your niche. Create a community or group where passionate discussions can take place.

7. **Niche Forums and Online Communities**: Participate in forums like Reddit or specialized online communities. Look for threads and discussions related to your product or service.

8. **Product Review Sites**: Monitor sites like Amazon, Yelp, or Trustpilot. Reach out to users who leave detailed, positive reviews.

9. **Events and Conventions**: Attend industry-specific events, trade shows, and conventions. Set-up a booth or sponsor a session to interact with potential superfans.

10. **Meetup Groups**: Join or create Meetup groups related to your product or service. Host events or workshops to connect with enthusiasts.

The last reason entrepreneurs choose the wrong customers is that they fail to see the difference between price customers and value customers. Price customers prioritize price above all things. You can add all the bells and whistles to your product or service, or even give them all the value in the world, and they still won't buy it. This is because the only thing price customers care about is getting the lowest price possible (think McDonalds or Walmart).

Value customers, on the other hand, appreciate the value you provide. And the more value you give them, the more they are willing to pay (think Nordstroms).

If you are all about creating value, you need to make sure you are only selling to value-based customers. You can recognize them because they are willing to pay more for more value you offer.

On the other hand, price customers are easily recognizable because the first question they will ask you is about the price and the discounts you can offer them. They will usually nickel and dime you until they get the product or service for almost free, then they will return it for a refund and give you a bad review.

If you are a value-based business then make sure you are selling to a value-based customer to avoid such a situation and get the sale every time.

The Value/Price Seesaw

Once you find your ideal customer, they might still not buy from you if they don't see enough value to justify the price.

This is because of the Value/Price Seesaw.

Imagine a seesaw. On one side of the seesaw, there is you. You are sitting on your side of the seesaw, sharing about your product and service, talking about all its features and benefits, and how much it will solve your customer's problems. Meanwhile, your potential customer is on the other side of the seesaw. They are weighed down by how little money they think they have, doubts that anyone can help them or fear that if they buy your product or service, it will let them down.

So your customer has all this weight pushing down on him or her. Meanwhile, you're talking about how great your product is as your legs are dangling in the air. As long as there is more weight on their side, there will never be a sale.

But then, you begin asking them about their problem and they start to feel that you understand what they are going through. As you take the time to listen, they begin to feel like you really care. Then you begin to educate them on the pains, challenges, and implications of not taking action. You show them how your product or service will help solve their exact problem, reducing, or sometimes, completely eliminating, their pain. Then you let them know that you'll give them their money back even if things don't work out. Suddenly, their side starts to become lighter (as they unload all their weight), and your side begins to get heavier because of the overwhelming value he or she sees your product or service will bring them. And this leads to a sale.

This metaphor shows the tug-of-war going on between the value you're communicating and your prospect's fears. A sale will only happen if your value exceeds your prospect's fears.

You can easily get the sale by either increasing the amount of value you bring to your customer or decreasing the amount of risk your customer is taking in purchasing your product or service, or both.

Therefore, by influencing the way they think, you can easily increase the perceived value of your offerings since both value and risk are in the customer's mind. And easily decrease the perceived risk of your offerings, making the sale a forgone conclusion.

So, you will be able to 100X your results and make the sale easily and effortlessly if you can 10X the value of your offerings, and reduce the risk by 10X for your customer.

Provide 10X as Much Value

If a sale is determined by the value you create, then your chance of getting the sale increases if you increase the amount of value. Increase the value by 10X, then the sale will be inevitable.

This is called Value Stacking—the more value you stack on your offers, the more your customer will believe your product is worth more than whatever price you are asking for, leading to a sale.

Now, the two main types of value you can stack on your offer are fixed value and dynamic value.

Fixed Value Stacking

Fixed value is the value you create when your product or service meets your buyers' exact needs, and their exact buying criteria.

The most important thing to your customer is whether your product or service can solve their main pain point. If your product or service cannot do this or does this weakly, it doesn't matter what other value you stack on your offer, the customer will not buy. But if you first identify the customers' main pain points, and then show them how your product or service matches what they are looking for perfectly, then that will create massive value and get you the sale.

For example, when Alex Hormozi would sell to customers looking to lose weight, he would identify his customer's exact pain points, like snacking habits, dislike for exercise, and maintaining motivation. He would then break down these challenges into more specific problems like difficulty in buying, preparing, and eating healthy food, and would then offer targeted solutions that would perfectly fit each of these areas. He would then focus on creating offerings that were so compelling and well-matched to the customer's needs that they felt an irresistible need to purchase them.

Reflection Checkpoint

Ask yourself:

1. Do my products and services meet all my customer's most important needs?
2. When was the last time that I asked them?

Buying Criteria

Another fixed value to consider is the customer's buying criteria. Every individual has a specific list of criteria that is important to them when purchasing. You will get the sale if you can identify these criteria, and then show how your product or service meets those criteria perfectly.

For example, if you have a customer whose three biggest buying criteria are price, quality, and ease of use—in that order—then you will need to match those criteria perfectly to get the sale.

If you find that you can't match these buying criteria because your product or service is expensive, you need to be flexible enough to adapt your offerings to meet their needs.

For example, let's say that your product is both high-quality and easy to use, but is expensive. You can offer the customer a payment plan to make the price easier to manage. Or you can provide an alternative product or service with fewer features for a lower price. Either way, when you adapt to the customer's buying criteria, you will get the sale.

And the simplest way to find out a buyer's buying criteria is to just ask. Asking, **"What are the three things that are most important to you when buying this product or service?"** is sufficient to give you the information you need to find solutions that match their buying criteria exactly.

Dynamic Value Stacking

Dynamic value are additional elements that the customer considers important that you can add to your offer to make it even more valuable. This is where you can really shine because the list of dynamic value you can stack is endless. The most important thing is that you get to know your prospect well so that you can identify what they value. Then stack as many of these value-creating options as you can, preferably in a way that is at a low cost to you.

Here is a quick list of dynamic value that you can provide to your prospective customer, that you can use in your sale meetings or marketing materials:

1. **Bonuses**: Include bonuses or additional services that complement the main offering.
2. **Adjustable Payment Plans**: Offer an easier or more convenient way to pay for the product or service.
3. **Quality**: Show evidence of high-quality materials, processes, or ingredients used.
4. **Future Proofing**: Explain how the product or service will remain relevant and valuable in the future.
5. **After-Sales Support**: Emphasize exceptional after-sales support and customer service.
6. **Training and Onboarding**: Offer comprehensive training and onboarding processes to ensure smooth implementation.
7. **Upgrades and Updates**: Offer information on future upgrades or updates to the product or service.
8. **Personalized Solutions**: Tailor the product or service to the specific needs of the prospect, showing a commitment to their unique requirements.
9. **Time Savings**: Show how the product or service can save time, a valuable resource for many customers.
10. **Environmental and Social Responsibility**: If applicable, highlight any eco-friendly aspects or social responsibility initiatives associated with the product or service.

The key is to identify what is important to your customer and add as much dynamic value as possible until the seesaw tips in your favor.

> ***For a list of many more ideas that will create value for your customer, try the 100X AI Business advisor for FREE here: 100xbusinessadvisor.ai.**

Reduce the Risk by 10X

Value can also be created by reducing the risk that the purchase of your product and service will bring to the customer.

Purchasing always carries risk. And the biggest risks your customers are thinking about include:

- "If I buy this product or service, will it really solve my problem or will it fail?"
- "If I buy this, is it worth not buying all the other things that I really need and want?"
- "Can I trust that the person selling me this product or service really cares about me, or are they just trying to take advantage of me?"

These kinds of risks lead to fear, and people will not take the risk of being hurt unless it is worth their while, or if you eliminate the fear, or both.

Therefore, increase the chances of getting the sale by adding more things to your offers that will reduce their risk. And if you remove 10X as much risk, it will almost guarantee the sale.

Here is a quick list of ways to reduce perceived risk for your prospective customer that you can use in your sales meetings or marketing materials:

1. **Money-Back Guarantee**: Offer a no-questions-asked refund policy to alleviate concerns about financial loss. If you really want to reduce risk even further, offer a double money back guarantee.
2. **Free Trial or Demo**: Provide a free trial period or live demonstration that allows prospects to experience the product or service without commitment.
3. **Customer Testimonials**: Share stories and endorsements from satisfied customers to build credibility and trust.
4. **Case Studies**: Use detailed case studies that demonstrate the product's effectiveness and return on investment for similar clients.
5. **Transparent Pricing**: Clearly explain pricing structures to avoid surprises, emphasizing value over cost.
6. **Warranty or Service Contracts**: Offer extended warranties or service contracts to cover potential future issues.
7. **Certifications and Awards**: Highlight any industry certifications, awards, or recognitions the product or service has received.
8. **Detailed Product Information**: Provide comprehensive product specifications and information to educate the prospect.
9. **Professional Associations**: Mention membership in professional associations to show industry commitment and standards.
10. **Risk-Sharing Arrangements**: Propose contracts that include risk-sharing clauses, such as payment upon achieving certain milestones.

*For a list of many more ideas that will reduce risk for your customer, try the 100X AI Business advisor for FREE here: 100xbusinessadvisor.ai.

The key is to identify the customers' biggest fears and risks and stack as many of these elements as possible to eliminate the risk. Then keep stacking, until, in their minds, the sale is a no-brainer.

For example, when we first started selling our binoculars to bird-watchers, we needed to build credibility in a really competitive market. So, we decided to provide a lifetime warranty for our products, giving customers the confidence that they could always get a replacement if things went wrong. This made the sale a no-brainer and gave some customers enough confidence to just buy the products for a test run, which is what we wanted.

We believed that once they tried them, they would buy them because the binoculars were so amazing. This allowed us to quickly become one of the premier birdwatching binocular companies in a very short time. After we built substantial credibility, we lowered the warranty to 12 months.

Go After 100X Customers

Another way to 100X your sales is to go after 100X customers.

Let's face it: there are people in the market who have 100X more money than everyone else. The good news is that these customers can be just as big superfans of your products and services as others. By targeting these individuals, you can charge them 10X as much and they will pay it because money is rarely an issue for these individuals. As a matter of fact, they won't see value in it unless it is worth 10X–100X more.

I found this out by accident when I substantially increased the price of one of our binoculars to stop people from purchasing them because we were low on inventory. Did it stop the purchasing? Not at all. People continued to buy the product, even now at triple the price. That showed me that there are people in the market who have a lot of money to spend, and will spend it, because if they see the value in your product or service, money is never an issue for them.

What is interesting is that many entrepreneurs get stuck in this area because they have two issues that have nothing to do with business, but more to do with a scarcity mindset.

Entrepreneurs overwhelmingly charge too little for their products and services because they don't believe anyone is willing to pay a high price for their products and services (which reveals that the entrepreneur doesn't believe it is worth that much either). Also, entrepreneurs go after the lower ends of the market, instead of charging 2X, 3X or even 10X more to get customers at the higher end of the market.

What is fascinating is that though there may be less people at the higher ends of the market, they are willing to spend substantially more.

If you go for the higher end of the market, you can get 10X greater returns, with 10X fewer customers to deal with, and less time, effort, resources, and money (TERM) to spend. In other words, 100X!

If you want to 100X your results, go after 100X customers.

Conclusion

Sales can be elusive, but it becomes easier to master once you understand that the key to all sales is creating value.

Like a seesaw, the key is to increase the amount of value you provide in your offer, while reducing risk for the customer. This will cause the seesaw to tip in your favor, and you will get the sale.

But first, you must make sure that you speak to the right prospective customers. The ideal customer will be the superfan who believes, respects, and sees great value in your products and services. Also they must be able to have plenty of money to purchase as well.

Once you find your ideal customer, provide such a compelling offer that it will be irresistible for prospective customers to say no. Give them 10X more value by value stacking, and reducing their risk by 10X.

And 10X times 10X = 100X!

Then, not only will you 100X your sales, but also 100X your returns because of all the highly motivated and happy customers you will have.

Now that you've learned how to multiply your sales, it's time to discuss how to deliver value to your customers in a way that leaves them highly satisfied but takes 100X less time and effort for you. If you are ready, then just turn the page to learn how to 100X your System.

ACTION STEPS

1. Consider your current product or service offer.
2. Add 10X more value to your offer by stacking value from the fixed and dynamic value list in this chapter.
3. Then reduce the risk of your offer by 10X through applying the risk-reducing ideas in this chapter.
4. Also, consider increasing your price substantially to attract customers at the high end of the market who can pay substantially more.

Pitfalls to Avoid

1. Make sure you provide value and reduce risk in a way that costs you little to no time, effort, resources, or money (TERM).

100X YOUR SYSTEM

"Everything should be made as simple as possible, but not simpler."
– Albert Einstein

Amancio Ortega Gaona, was born on March 28, 1936, in Busdongo de Arbás, Spain. Ortega's early life was marked by financial hardship. Born into a working-class family, his father was a railway worker, and his mother worked as a housemaid. This modest upbringing played a significant role in shaping his life and future in business. He left school at 14 to work as a shop hand for a local shirtmaker, where he learned the basics of clothing production and retail.

In 1963, Ortega started Confecciones Goa, selling quilted bathrobes. This was his first venture into the apparel industry, and it laid the groundwork for his future success. His business model was based on producing affordable clothing quickly and responding rapidly to new trends.

In 1975, Ortega opened his first fashion store, called Zara, near his first workshop. Ortega's unique approach offered fashion-forward clothing at reasonable prices. He achieved this by controlling most of the production and supply chain instead of using the traditional fashion production model, allowing for rapid turnaround from design to available in-store.

This became known as "fast fashion"—a term that describes the rapid movement of high fashion designs to the retail floor.

Zara's growth was nothing short of phenomenal. Zara stores were a fixture in Spain by the 1980s, and the 1990s saw the brand's international expansion.

Ortega's approach resulted in disrupting the traditional fashion industry. His model was based on frequent, small-batch deliveries to stores, significantly shortening the fashion cycle. Unlike traditional retailers that restock only a few times a season, Zara restocks new designs twice a week. This created a sense of scarcity and urgency among customers, boosting sales.

Zara's impact on the fashion world also challenged the notion that quality and style could only come from high-end fashion brands. Zara brought trendy, designer-inspired fashion to the masses, making it accessible and affordable.

Amancio Ortega's creation of a fast fashion model with Zara revolutionized the retail fashion industry, and made current trends quickly and widely accessible, while also influencing how the fashion retail industry operated.

Getting Back to First Principles

Ortega's approach to business is a great example of taking a traditional, overburdened system and reducing it to its most important components. Zara revolutionized the fashion industry by taking the traditional fashion production system, dismantling it, and then redesigning it in a way that optimized speed and value to customers.

This is a great example of **First Principles Thinking**. First principles thinking is a method that involves breaking down complex systems into basic elements and then reassembling them from the ground up for greater effectiveness and efficiency. It's about questioning assumptions and conventions to create original solutions, multiply impact, while eliminating waste.

As a fast fashion brand, Zara optimized their offerings in several key ways:

1. **Speed to Market**: The production of new styles from the drawing board to the store happened within a few weeks. This is much faster than the previous approach where new styles were only released every season.
2. **Supply Chain Control:** They handled their supply chains themselves. This let them react quickly and stay in control. Traditional fashion brands used to depend on multiple different suppliers.
3. **Inventory Management:** They brought in small shipments often. This helps them avoid having too much stock and keeps their items fresh. This is different from the traditional method where big orders were made each season.

4. **Product Variety and Limited Availability:** Continuously updating their products, making customers feel like they need to buy quickly. This is different from traditional fashion, which only had a few new styles each season.
5. **Smart Pricing:** They kept their prices steady. They did this by quickly adapting to what customers want and managing their stock well. This is different from traditional fashion, which often had to discount prices at the end of a season.
6. **Following Trends Quickly:** They brought the latest high fashion trends to the mass market quickly. This happened much faster than with traditional retailers, who had a considerable lag time.

In a similar example, Elon Musk often cites first principles thinking as key to his approach at SpaceX and Tesla. Instead of following the traditional methods, he deconstructed problems to their fundamentals (like the raw materials cost of a battery, or necessary components in rockets) and then found more innovative and cost-effective solutions.

Musk's first principles approach revolutionized space travel by substantially lowering the cost and reducing the time to launch. For instance, a single Space Shuttle launch was estimated to cost around $450 million to $1.5 billion. In contrast, SpaceX's Falcon 9 rocket, which is partially reusable, has a price tag of about $62 million per launch.

Another well-known example was the McDonald brothers' efforts to redesign their original BBQ restaurant to remain competitive in the restaurant business. They simplified their menu to the smallest amount of food items to sell—burgers, fries, and drinks. They also changed their way of serving food to an assembly line model to improve speed, efficiency, and simplicity.

The resulting shorter wait times, faster service and cheaper food was a hit, and the McDonald's Speedee system was born. This same system paved the way for the current 600-billion-dollar modern fast-food industry we have today.

It's Time to Upgrade Your System

Entrepreneurs in today's marketplace are realizing that it is not enough to bring a product to market and sell as many products as possible. Competition is so strong and fierce that they are constantly taking bites out of your market share and gaining speed, trying to overtake you.

Also, competition is operating leaner and faster, so entrepreneurs don't have room to operate in an overcomplicated, bloated and cost heavy way. The lack of speed and efficiency only slows you down, giving your competition ample time to catch up to you.

Entrepreneurs are also realizing there is no room for spending substantial amount of time, effort, resources, and money (TERM) with little to no return to show for their efforts. This is the unfortunate state that many entrepreneurs are finding themselves in today.

Too many entrepreneurs are experiencing the all-too-common pattern of putting in long work hours, making large capital investments, building large teams, but have little to no profits to show for their efforts at the end of the day.

So what's the answer?

Taking a lesson from Zara's example, the answer lies in streamlining your operations to their simplest and leanest form so you can operate with 10X less TERM and consistently bring 10X more value to customers.

In other words, if you want to 100X your results, it's time to 100X Your System.

Reducing Your System By 10X

Kaizen states that all systems have room to improve and have waste that needs to be eliminated. Parkinson's Law says that the time you give to something is the time it will take to do something. Occam's Razor says that the simpler the solution, the better it is. And First Principles thinking says that there is more value in breaking down an operation to its simplest form and building from there.

These 4 principles reveal that right now, the bloated systems we are using to bring value to customers can be substantially shaved down, so we can operate leaner, without reducing the quality of our products and services.

In other words, there are many areas in your business that are not bringing value, but that are wasting valuable TERM. Not only are they wasting resources, but they are also a distraction from your main goal of providing great value to customers.

Those valuable resources could be put to better use elsewhere, especially toward areas that are bringing large results. And if you can reclaim these wasted resources, you can even pass some of them back to your customers, creating more value, and making you even more competitive.

I experienced this in my previous career as a business consultant. When I began my career, I was working 6 long days a week, while feeling like I wasn't accomplishing everything I needed to get done. But then I decided to put these principles to the test. I started reducing the days I worked from 6 days a week to 5 days. Then to 4, then 3, then 2 and then finally 1 day a week. Before I left that career, I was working 1 day a week, providing much higher value to my clients, and making more money than I was when I was working 6 days a week.

I also experienced this in our birdwatching binoculars business. When I started the business, I decided that I would keep shaving it down to its simplest form, so that I could provide high value to my customers with little effort.

Some of the things I did included:

- Using Amazon's fulfillment services to take care of our fulfillment and returns.
- Hired a trained logistics person to manage inventory, and a customer service rep to take care of all our customer service needs.
- Outsourced our sales tax collections and filing to an expert.
- Automated as many repetitive tasks as I could find.
- Negotiated with our supplier to send our inventory directly to Amazon, taking us out of the equation.

By the time I had finished shaving off the unnecessary tasks off our system, I was working only 15 minutes a week, selling millions of dollars in inventory. Also, recently, I've got it down now to only working 15 minutes a month.

Reflection Checkpoint

1. What are areas in your business that can operate more efficiently?
2. What steps can you take today to start operating leaner?

Reducing your operations by 10X takes deliberate focus and effort. The opportunities are there, but it won't happen on its own unless you make it a priority to keep operating leaner. But if you don't, just know that your competitor is smart enough to see the value of being more efficient, and they will devote the time to becoming leaner and taking your business.

If you don't want to be left behind, it's time to start cutting out the excess fat in your system and start operating leaner.

Here are a few ideas to help you create a routine to operate leaner:

Remove 10 Steps From Your System

Schedule time monthly to evaluate your main systems and consider 10 steps you can remove from each of them. Those items could be unnecessary steps that are a normal part of the process, but once removed, allow you to operate leaner without reducing quality. Or you can change the order of the system, and you might discover you can do it using fewer parts. Or you can remove some access to the system to parties who don't bring value to it but are adding extra steps in communication.

You can do this for customers also. If the features of a product or service you're providing do not bring customers value, remove it. It will save you money in providing it, and since it's of little value to customers, they won't notice, or they may even appreciate you simplifying it. Also, if there are customers that are providing little value, but you are still spending a lot of resources on them, let them go and refer them to your competitor instead.

The key to reducing 10 steps effectively is consistency. It is not something that you do once, but you need to make it a routine to do it monthly or every few weeks. This way, every few weeks, you are making your operation leaner, and more effective, while still providing great value to customers.

Here are a few ideas of things you can remove to quickly make your operation leaner:

1. **Try a Shorter Workweek**: Surprisingly, working less can make your team more focused, productive, happier, and might even cut down on how much it costs to run your business.
2. **Crowdsource Ideas:** Save time by using online platforms to gather ideas, solve problems, or get small tasks done, like creating a logo or handling your social media.
3. **Keep Inventory Just-in-Time:** Adopt a system where you only order inventory when needed, reducing the cost of storing goods.

4. **Trade Services with Other Businesses:** Look for opportunities to swap services with other companies. This can help save some cash and forge strong connections with other companies.

5. **Use Zero Based Budgeting:** Instead of using last year's expenses as a starting point, plan your budget from zero. Question every expense to avoid unnecessary spending.

6. **Choose Open Source Software**: Cut out expensive commercial software and instead consider using free, open-source software.

7. **Train Customers to Help Themselves:** Reduce effort servicing customers by setting up online tools or chatbots so customers can find answers or get help on their own.

8. **Let Customers Help Design Products:** Reduce design time by involving your customers when making something new. You can ask them what they think through surveys, let them try out products early, and listen to their suggestions.

9. **Start a Skill Sharing Program:** Reduce training time by motivating your employees to share their special skills with each other. This is a good way to get better at different things without having to pay for training, and it helps everyone work together more smoothly.

10. **Team Up for Marketing:** Reduce marketing budget spend by working with other businesses who aren't your competitors on marketing projects. This can cut your marketing costs in half while helping you reach twice as many people.

Challenge Assumptions

We assume that the steps we take are necessary only because we've been doing them for so long. The key is to have a justifiable reason for every step in your system so that you are not taking unnecessary steps and wasting resources.

Question every part of a system and find out the purpose for the step and if it's worth keeping.

Go through your entire operational system and ask, **"What value is this step bringing to our customers or our business?"**

If it is not bringing a justifiable value, remove it.

But just remember, "This is the way we've always done it," is not a justifiable reason.

Do Things In-House if it Brings You More Value

I believe that most things in an organization can be outsourced and should be. But, if there are high-value items that benefit from your control, then bring it in-house. For example, if you benefit more by having your design and development done in-house, because you have more control and can turn around products faster, then it will be wise to invest in hiring a designer and developer. Or like in Zara's example, they had more access to determine their design schedule and turnaround time because they controlled their in-house supply chain.

Because of the high value these bring to your business, it's worth the investment even though it may cost more money upfront.

Upgrade your System by 10X

Another way you can multiply value is by adding highly valuable steps to your system. These are small steps that don't require a lot of time and resources, but bring a high level of value to your customers and business.

For example, Zara's fast fashion model gave them the space to continuously introduce new products, creating a constantly evolving range of choices. This strategy catered to a consumer desire for variety and created a sense of scarcity and urgency to purchase, as items were not guaranteed to be restocked.

Zara also introduced greater and quicker access to new trends, seen in high fashion or popular culture, making them available to the mass market while they were still highly relevant.

The good news is that many of these options didn't cost much to provide, and even if some did, the cost was covered by the savings they received from cutting out expensive and unnecessary steps in the traditional fashion production system.

In developing binocular products for birdwatchers, we saved on costs by operating lean and put some of that money saved toward creating more innovative binocular designs that brought a lot of value to our customers. We could afford higher quality glass lenses, giving birdwatchers an HD experience, increasing the value for the customer, and allowing us to increase the price. Eventually, we sold so much inventory that the supplier covered the cost of these innovations so that we could bring greater value to customers at no cost to us.

The key to adding valuable steps to your system is that it must produce **substantial value for your customers** and **more profit** for you, while using the **least amount of resources**.

For example, this could be as simple as:

- Setting a time for asking for referrals at the end of your client meetings.
- Automatically sending birthday cards to your customers to build stronger loyalty.
- Adding an upsell request script for every customer service call.

Though simple, these small additions have the potential to greatly multiply your returns.

Here is a list of other small steps you can add to your business systems, which combined, can add a lot of value to your business:

1. Implement a **post-purchase follow-up email** sequence to gather feedback and encourage repeat business.
2. Introduce a **customer loyalty program** with rewards for frequent purchases.
3. Add an **AI chat feature** on your website to provide instant customer support, make more sales and increase engagement.
4. Create a **referral program** with incentives for customers who bring in new business.
5. **Automate** sending invoice reminders to ensure timely payments and improve cash flow.
6. Develop a system for **regular check-ins with high-value clients** to strengthen relationships and identify upsell opportunities.

7. Integrate **cross-selling and upselling** suggestions into your e-commerce checkout process.
8. Use **customer segmentation** to personalize marketing messages and offers.
9. Offer a **discount or bonus** to customers who prepay for services or buy in bulk.
10. Set-up **automated birthday or anniversary greetings** with special offers to enhance customer loyalty.

Each of these small steps can lead to improved customer satisfaction, increased sales, and better operational efficiency. Combined, they bring 10X more value to your customers and business.

> ***For many more ideas for simple steps that can add significant value to your system, try the 100X AI Business Advisor for FREE here: 100xbusinessadvisor.ai.**

Conclusion

Every business has room to improve. The more you devote the time to streamline your operation and operate in a leaner way:

- The **greater profits** you can keep.
- The **faster** you will move in the market.
- The **more value** you will bring to customers.
- The **greater the edge** you will have over your competition.

You can do this by reducing your operation by 10X, systematically shaving the amount of time, effort, resources, and money (TERM) you spend to deliver value to your customers. You can also do this by consistently adding more valuable steps to your operation that will create 10X more value for your customers and your business.

This way you will 100X your system and 100X your business results by increasing your value by 10X and operating leaner using 10X less TERM. Now it's time to turn the page to learn how to attract the kind of team members that will easily multiply your results by 100X.

ACTION STEPS

1. Set-up a time to review your main operating system.
2. Go through your main operational system and practice removing 10 steps.
3. Then add 10 simple steps that add value and increase the profits in your business.
4. Do it again every month or quarter.

Pitfalls to Avoid

1. As you simplify and remove items, don't go too simple.
2. Avoid simplifying to the point that you lose quality or reduce the value you bring to customers.

100X YOUR TEAM

"One extraordinary talent can provide the spark that ignites the fire of excellence in a team."

– Unknown

In 1996, Apple Computer Inc. faced a dire financial situation, marking one of the lowest points in the company's history. In its fiscal year ending in September 1996, the company reported a loss of $816 million, one of its biggest annual losses ever. This was a stark contrast to the profitable and innovative company Apple had been in the 1980s and early 1990s.

Apple's sales were declining rapidly. The company's market share had shrunk considerably, falling to around 4% of the global PC market. This decline was due to intense competition from PCs running Microsoft's Windows 95 operating system that offered lower prices and a wider range of software options.

Several of Apple's product launches at that time were also unsuccessful. Products such as the Apple Newton—an early attempt at a handheld device—failed to gain significant market traction. The Macintosh Performa, aimed at the consumer market, also underperformed due to its high price and the confusing number of models.

The company had also had several CEOs in a short period, and none had been able to reverse Apple's misfortunes. There was a lack of consistent leadership and vision, which was critical in a rapidly evolving technology market. The company's poor performance also led to low employee morale and a demoralized culture.

Apple had all the makings of a case study in bankruptcy.

Steve Jobs' return to Apple in 1997 marked the beginning of a remarkable turnaround for the company.

When he returned to Apple, Steve Jobs initiated a strategic overhaul by refocusing the company's product line. He dramatically streamlined Apple's offerings, reducing the number of models, and shifting the focus to fewer, more refined products.

Jobs also worked to rebuild Apple's brand, focusing on creating a premium image and developing an effective marketing strategy. The "Think Different" campaign, launched in 1997, repositioned Apple as a brand for creative and unconventional individuals.

Yet, one of the best decisions that truly catapulted Apple to a new level of technological achievement is what Steve Jobs did next. Initially a member of the design team, Jony Ive's talents were not immediately recognized. Apple's significant internal turmoil and market challenges affected the design department's influence.

However, Ive's fortunes changed dramatically when Steve Jobs gave Ive's greater freedom and responsibility, marking the beginning of a partnership that would define an era in technology design.

Their collaboration led to the creation of groundbreaking products such as the iMac in 1998, which was pivotal in reviving Apple's brand. This success was followed by other iconic designs such as the iPod (2001), iPhone (2007), MacBook Air (2008), iPad (2010), and later, the Apple Watch (2015), each reshaping its respective market.

With one strategic move to partner with a talented individual like Jony Ive, Steve Jobs laid the foundation for Apple to become the first company in history to reach a trillion-dollar valuation.

It's Time to Upgrade Your Team

As entrepreneurs, if there is one thing that we can all agree on, it's that business struggles are common.

Like right now, you may be:

- Facing struggles getting your business off the ground.
- Experiencing your growth curve turning in the wrong direction.
- Having trouble getting customers.
- Having stagnant sales because your competition is chomping away at your market share.

The good news is that despite all these struggles, Jony Ive's story is a reminder that you may be only one hire away from 100X growth in your business.

Reflection Checkpoint

1. On a scale of 1–10 (10 being greatest), in your business, how much impact has each team member brought to your team?
2. What can you do to help them improve?

Having the right people in your organization is one of the greatest determiners of success in business. This is because some people have so much talent, energy, character, positivity, and integrity that they are 100X more productive, 100X easier to work with, and can create 100X more value than average individuals.

These high-value team members:

- Have built **solid character** and produced great results during their career.
- Are also **growth-minded** and **adaptable** to what is needed to get the job done, no matter how difficult. **Have ambition** and **drive** to accomplish more, which usually results in consistent, excellent, and effective work.

I experienced this when I was lucky enough to meet my book designer, Adina. I contracted Adina to help me design my first book over 10 years ago. Her talent, attention to detail, hard work ethic and consistent excellent work, has made her my go-to designer for all my books, including this one.

Working with Adina has taught me one powerful lesson that has been one of the biggest keys that has allowed me to 100X my results in my various endeavors. That lesson is: in your entrepreneurship journey, you need to collect phenomenal, talented, hardworking people, and never let them go.

In other words, if you want to 100X your results, you need to 100X your team.

Now, you may be asking yourself, "Where can I find these special people, and how can I get them on my team fast?!?!" And more importantly, "How am I going to pay them?"

The good news is that it is a lot easier than you think.

Here are a few things you can start doing immediately to find and work with these special people, so you can quickly begin to 100X your results.

10X Your Hiring Criteria

The criteria you currently use to pick your team is probably the reason why you're not attracting the best talent. It's no longer acceptable to hire someone referred to you by a friend or family member, or to hire the first person to apply, or hire your cousin, or the cheapest contractor.

If you want to upgrade your team, then the standard for hiring needs to change to ONLY hiring the best.

Who are the best? The best are:

1. Contractors with **4 1/2-star ratings with thousands of reviews** from satisfied customers.
2. **Talented people** who have worked for high-level organizations for years and have received nothing but great recommendations.
3. **Hardworking and effective team members** who have been tested, and they can show you proof of the millions of dollars in value they have produced for others.
4. Professionals with **glowing endorsements** from high level people you know and trust.
5. Experts with a ton of rewards, trophies, and **recognition for their work** because they've earned it.

If you want to upgrade your team, these are the people you need to decide to only allow in your organization from now on. (Which also means you need to be ready to fire a lot of average people on your team as soon as possible.)

Consider using the following hiring checklist to evaluate anyone that is interested in being part of your team and make sure that they embody these qualities:

1. **Integrity:**
   - Conduct thorough background checks
   - Ask for specific examples during interviews where candidates demonstrated integrity
   - Request references and speak with them, focusing on integrity-related questions

2. Proactivity:

- Look for a history of self-started projects or initiatives in their resume
- Ask candidates to describe situations where they took initiative beyond their job requirements
- Evaluate their approach to problem-solving and whether they anticipate challenges

3. Energy Level:

- Observe their enthusiasm and stamina during the interview process
- Inquire about their interests and activities outside of work to gauge energy levels
- Consider a work trial or a project-based assessment to see their energy in action

4. Resourcefulness:

- Present hypothetical work scenarios to assess their ability to think on their feet
- Ask about times they've overcome obstacles with limited resources
- Evaluate their ability to leverage networks and tools to solve problems

5. Work Ethic:

- Ask for examples of when they went above and beyond their job duties
- Discuss their views on work-life balance to understand their commitment levels
- Look for a consistent track record of delivering results

6. **Talent:**
   - Ensure their skills and experiences align with the job requirements
   - Use skill assessments or practical tasks to evaluate their proficiency
   - Discuss their past achievements and how they reached them to understand their talents and capabilities

10X Your Business Culture

Now, if you're worried about how you're going to pay these special individuals to get them to work with you, you need to start by understanding how these special individuals think. You see, high-level team members value a lot more things than just money.

They value:

- Growth opportunities
- Challenging and fulfilling work
- Responsibility
- A strong purpose

By upgrading your culture to a 10X level, these individuals will be pushing the door down to work for your organization because this is the type of environment they desire, and believe they deserve to be part of. Also, because high-value cultures are rare, people everywhere will hear about it when you create this type of culture.

People will leave a high paying job if their environment does not fulfill them. The opposite is also true—people are willing to work for less (temporarily) if their environment provides fulfilling work, growth opportunities, and a purpose.

Devote time to build a high integrity, growth-oriented, empathetic, purpose-driven culture. It will attract these special individuals and make them loyal to you for years.

Eventually, these individuals will help you multiply your returns in a very short time and you can reward them handsomely for their contribution. This will make them even more loyal to you, creating an ever-growing cycle of productivity, rewards, and growth.

Attracting 100X Level Team Members

If you don't have a lot of money to hire these special individuals, but you want to attract high-value talent, it will take focusing on creating an environment that offers the kind of benefits that resonate deeply with these team members' intrinsic motivations.

Here are some examples of non-monetary ways to attract and incentivize such talent:

1. **Learning Programs for Employees:** Start programs that let employees learn new things and gain skills matching their interests and career plans.
2. **Chances to Lead:** Give employees the opportunity to oversee projects. This can help them grow and feel proud and connected to their work.
3. **A Culture of New Ideas:** Create an environment where everyone is encouraged to suggest new ideas and work on the latest projects.

4. **Balancing Work and Personal Life:** Support employees in having a good balance between work and their personal lives, and include policies such as unlimited paid time off.

5. **Meaningful Work:** Make sure everyone understands how their job helps achieve the company's goals and makes a positive difference for customers or the community.

6. **Welcoming All Backgrounds:** Build a workplace that appreciates diversity and inclusion, making sure everyone feels respected and valued for what they bring to the table.

7. **Taking Care of Employee Health:** Have programs aimed at keeping employees both mentally and physically healthy, such as mindfulness practices, fitness classes at work, or offering healthy snacks.

8. **Contributing to Social Causes:** Get involved in efforts that matter to your employees, such as protecting the environment or supporting social justice.

9. **Open Communication:** Keep the lines of communication open between bosses and employees, so everyone feels like they have a voice and are up-to-date on what's happening in the company.

10. **Special Benefits:** Offer special benefits that make everyday life better or easier, such as childcare at work, allowing pets in the office, or help with travel costs.

For highly talented and purpose-driven individuals, creating a culture full of these benefits will compensate them enough that they will be willing to work for less money or accept flexible compensation packages. Yet, with their help, you will be able to quickly begin to 100X your results, helping you to compensate them more and more as time goes on.

Conclusion

Right now, you are one hire away from making a 100X jump in your business. This is because there are special individuals in the marketplace whose character, talent, integrity, and work ethic allows them to magnify your efforts. Together with you, and a team of other high-value individuals, you can create a synergy of exponential impact for years to come.

You need to 10X your hiring criteria to attract these individuals and filter out anyone else besides the best-in-class individuals who are a great fit for your company. Then you need to 10X your culture as well, so that their deep needs for purpose, growth and fulfilling work are met, and they can feel fully compensated with more than just money.

So if you 10X your hiring criteria, and 10X your culture, you will create a 100X team that will 100X your business results.

Now that you have the training to find the best people to bring into your business it's time to find the network of people outside of your business who can continually bring you the most 100X opportunities so you can 100X your results. To learn how, just turn the page, because that's the subject of our next chapter.

ACTION STEPS

1. Create a hiring checklist using the hiring criteria in this chapter.
   a. Only hire those that fit all the criteria.
   b. Though it will take some time to find them, do not compromise on these criteria.

2. Conduct a feedback survey for all your team members and ask them how your company culture rates on the following qualities, and make an effort to improve them:
   a. High integrity
   b. Empathetic
   c. Growth-oriented
   d. Purpose-driven
   e. Fulfilling and challenging work

3. Begin implementing the non-monetary programs from the list in this chapter that meet your team's deeper needs.

Pitfalls to Avoid

1. Avoid rushing the hiring process and make sure to thoroughly vet candidates. And don't compromise on the checklist!
2. Look for compatibility and cultural fit. Don't just focus solely on skills and experience.
3. Avoid making the hiring decision alone. Make sure to get multiple people's opinions throughout the hiring process.

100X YOUR NETWORK

"You are the average of the five people you spend the most time with."
—Jim Rohn

A geeky college undergrad and a serial entrepreneur walk into a bar. Or that is close to how a serendipitous encounter turned into one of the greatest success stories in history.

In the summer of 2004, this geeky undergrad, Mark Zuckerberg, took a trip to New York City to work on an algorithm for a peer-to-peer file-sharing application. He was invited to a party, and while there, struck up a conversation with Sean Parker, co-founder of Napster and a well-known figure in the tech industry.

They began talking, and despite Zuckerberg's initial unfamiliarity with Parker, they quickly found common ground. They discussed their shared interests in technology and the future of the internet.

Parker's charisma and his knowledge of the social dynamics of the internet resonated with Zuckerberg. Parker could articulate a vision for Facebook that went beyond its current function as a college networking site. Parker saw Facebook as a platform that could revolutionize the way people connected with each other on a global scale. He also advised Zuckerberg to drop "The" from "The Facebook," making the brand more accessible and universal.

Sean Parker's influence on Zuckerberg was significant. Parker's experience with startups and the tech industry was invaluable in helping the young Zuckerberg learn the ropes. Parker was also instrumental in shaping the company's early culture and business strategy. He became Facebook's first President, guided its expansion, developed its revenue models, and navigated the complex landscape of Silicon Valley.

Parker's deep understanding of the social dynamics of the internet and his experience with the legal and business challenges faced by Napster were also invaluable in steering Facebook during its early stages.

Parker also played a pivotal role in helping Facebook receive its first major investment. He introduced Zuckerberg to Peter Thiel, co-founder of PayPal, who became Facebook's first outside investor, injecting $500,000 into the company.

Sean Parker's meeting with Mark Zuckerberg was a turning point for Facebook. Parker brought to the table his experience, network, and vision, which were crucial in transforming Facebook from a college networking site into a global phenomenon.

The Power of High-Value People

Sean Parker's influence on Mark Zuckerberg is a great example of the power that an influential peer group can have on your life and business.

So, if you've ever found yourself:

- Working hard but you still haven't made the progress you want toward reaching your financial goals.
- Or after years of blood, sweat and tears, your business is still not getting the returns you hoped for.
- Or you're racking your brain trying to understand why you're only making 5–6 figures, instead of 7 or 8.

Then it is probably because of one thing.

Your peer group.

This is because the greatest influence of how much your business will grow is how much you as an individual grows. And one of the greatest determiners of how much any individual grows is their peer group.

Reflection Checkpoint

1. Who are you spending most of your time with?
2. Are most of them where you want to be?

Your Center of Influence Network (COIN)

Your peer group or network is the group of people you:

- Spend most of your time with
- Get the most advice from
- Bounce ideas off of
- Connect with
- Do business with
- Bring value to

You create the most synergy with these people, leading to everyone mutually benefiting from the relationship.

Having a high-level peer group also means surrounding yourself with individuals who will give you the highest quality advice. These individuals are bold enough to challenge your thinking and call you out on your excuses. Because of their influence, your network will also open doors for you and even do business with you, greatly multiplying your results.

For example, Sean Parker's influence at the right time in Mark Zuckerberg's career was critical to giving him the advice, support, resources, and connections he needed to take Facebook to the next level in its growth. Eventually, Zuckerberg surpassed Parker and saw the value of finding other mentors to help him grow in his leadership and further shape the trajectory of Facebook as a company. Some notable mentors included Peter Thiel, Steve Jobs, Don Graham, Bill Gates, and Marc Andreesen.

Unfortunately, the opposite is also true. If most of your time is spent isolated or surrounded by people who are constantly getting advice from you, you will eventually stop growing. This is because you are not being challenged and you stop learning, increasing your chances of stumbling and decreasing your chances of success.

Like Michael Dell said, "If you're the smartest person in the room, then you need to find another room."

Or worse, if you are surrounded by people with different values who don't believe in your vision or don't see the value in your ambitions, their criticisms and opposition will be a burdensome weight preventing you from reaching escape velocity (aka: your full potential).

My point is that if you want to 100X your results, your center of influence network (COIN) will give you the greatest 100X boost upward. But surrounding yourself with the wrong peer group will guarantee your plummet downward. So you need to choose your peer group carefully.

In other words, if you want to 100X your results, you need to 100X your network.

3 Types of People

Which individuals will 100X your network and lead to catapulting your results by 100X?

There are three types of people who you can choose to build your network—the isolated, the interested, and the influential.

The Isolated

Isolated people are those who tend to have little influence on others' lives. They will do their job and do it well, but they see little value in establishing relationships other than those they need to accomplish what they need to do.

This describes many entrepreneurs who are introverts by nature and tend to work from home, spending 90% of their time alone in front of a computer. When they must interact with the outside world, they will send an email or text (their favorite communication method), and then retreat to their isolation.

Though I don't like to admit it, by nature, this probably describes me the best. It takes a mammoth amount of effort for me to devote time and effort to spend time influencing others, and even when I'm doing it, I'm hoping it will end quickly so I can retreat back into isolation. I'm sure many of my fellow introverts who are reading this can relate.

The obvious challenge is that since our business results are greatly multiplied based on the amount of 100X people we are around, then we need to force ourselves to build these influential relationships. We either need to practice becoming ambiverts (both introverted and extroverted). Or be willing to practice becoming "shotgun extroverts," putting out energy for 2 hours at a time but then scheduling retreat time in between to isolate and recharge.

The Interested

The interested are those that have some influence on the lives of people in their life, but only a few in their inner circle. These are the type of people that do their job, but they generally need time to blow off steam by spending time with friends, and find great pleasure in connecting with others.

The good news is that these types of individuals generally know some influential people because these types of people are usually part of an influencer's fan base. They are the subscribers, members, followers, etc. that make up the largest section of an influencer's network. They are a great source for introductions to influential people—though they may not have as much influence.

The Influential

You know the influential because of the number of people in their circle that trust their advice and act on it. They make suggestions and thousands of people act on their advice and continue to do so because of the trust these influencers have built with them and the results these influential people bring to their lives.

Often people confuse being influential with being popular. The truth is that popularity does not equal influence because people do not seek advice on important areas of their lives from popular people. Rather, they go to popular people for entertainment, and maybe influence in minor areas, but not for guidance in crucial areas of their life.

Influential people generally influence those in the Interested or the Isolated group. They have thousands or even millions of these fans, and they influence their buying decisions, perspectives, political affiliations and more.

Therefore, building relationships with influencers can greatly multiply your returns because that one relationship will be multiplied
among thousands of their followers. 80% of your efforts needs to be
devoted to this group of people, if you want to multiply your results.

Reflection Checkpoint

1. Which category describes you the best (the isolated, interested, influential)?
2. Who do you spend time with most?

Influencing the Influencers

Even more powerful than influencers, are the influencers that
influence the influencers. This is who you need to become if you
want to 100X your results.

In my experience meeting with and influencing influencers, the
one consistent pattern I see is that influencers are human just like
me, and they have problems that need to be solved just like I do.

What I mean by this is that influencers have a personality, with
values that are important to them, perspectives they believe in, and
opinions they hold. They also want what most people want, which
is fulfilling their purpose in life and building a happy, fulfilling life
for them and their loved ones.

Knowing this helps me to relate to and connect with them on a
human level by being a great listener and offering my support. This

leads to building a lot of trust with them, making my influence with them even stronger.

Influential people are purpose-driven, ambitious people, and run into obstacles in reaching their vision like the rest of us. And just like us, they need advice, guidance, support, accountability, inspiration, and help.

For me, this gives me the opportunity to use my resources to help them fix their problem, increasing my value in their eyes. And once they see the value our relationship brings them over a period of time, my ability to influence them grows even more.

I also try my best to become good friends with these individuals, and not just treat them like a business colleague. Success is a lonely place for influential people. Few people think at their level so there are few people to share their crazy vision and ideas with.

Therefore, I make every effort to not only be there for business help and support, but also to be a friend as well. This goes a long way in growing my influence in their lives, especially because I start to truly care for them, and I want to bring them benefit them in some way.

Choosing Your Center of Influence Network

If you want to 100X your network, your peer group needs to have influential people from all walks of life. The greater the variety of people in your life, the more opportunities you open yourself to that you wouldn't otherwise have access to.

For example, besides having business and technological advisors, Bill Gates was instrumental in helping Mark Zuckerberg explore and increase his philanthropic work. Gate's commitment to philanthropy reinforced Zuckerberg's own desire to use his wealth and influence for positive social impact.

Here is a list of people you can choose from that would be highly valuable to have in your center of influence network and where you can find them:

1. **Industry Influencers**: Attend industry conferences, join professional associations, and engage on social media platforms like LinkedIn and Twitter.
2. **Venture Capitalists**: Network at investment forums, startup meetups, and through online investor platforms.
3. **Strategic Business Partners**: Look for complementary businesses and reach out for collaboration opportunities through B2B networking events.
4. **High Net-Worth Clients**: Join exclusive clubs, attend charity events, and participate in high-end networking groups.
5. **Suppliers and Vendors**: Attend trade shows, industry-specific expos, and use B2B marketplaces.
6. **Government Officials**: Engage in local business chambers, attend town hall meetings, and participate in public-private partnership initiatives.
7. **Thought Leaders**: Connect through TEDx events, speaker series, and academic conferences.
8. **Technology Innovators**: Visit tech hubs, innovation labs, and participate in hackathons.
9. **Marketing Gurus**: Engage with marketing forums, digital marketing conferences, and social media groups.

10. **Non-Profit Leaders**: Volunteer, sponsor events, and join boards of non-profits in your industry or community.

*For a list of many more high-value people to have as part of your center of influence network, try the 100X AI Business Advisor for FREE here: 100xbusinessadvisor.ai.

The more of these individuals make up your network, the greater your influence will multiply in various industries and walks of life.

Reflection Checkpoint

1. Go on social media and find an influencer you really admire.
2. Send them a direct message or email and let them know who you are, and how much you appreciate their work. Then ask them if you could either interview them or discuss how you can work together.

Now let's discuss how to begin creating a network full of influential people.

Spend Time with 10X More Influencers

The more time you spend with high-value influencers, the more you will become like them. Therefore, filling your schedule with meetings with these people will impact your life and business the most.

If you are like most entrepreneurs, you are so busy that you usually meet maybe 1 or 2 influential people a month. If you want to multiply your returns, then you need to multiply that list by 10X.

At a minimum, you should have 2–3 appointments with high-value people a week. And eventually consider increasing that number to 5–6 influential people a week.

Why so many? Because these individuals will have the most rapid, large-scale impact on multiplying your business efforts. They will help you focus on where you can get the biggest returns by leveraging their expertise, experience, and their own network. Not to mention many of these people will bring you considerably more customers, sales, and opportunities.

Therefore if you want to multiply your results, begin scheduling 2–3 meetings a week with these individuals and eventually get up to 5–6 a week.

Bring Them 10X More Value

The greater value you bring to these individuals, the greater your influence will grow. So you must make your meetings worth their while.

- If they have a problem, then turn the world upside down and help them fix it.
- If there is a connection they want to make, use your resources to help them make it.
- If they need a resource, work with your network to help them find it.

By solving their problems in this way, you will become a valuable partner and resource for them, and they will happily return the favor.

One thing about influential, high-value people is that they are very generous. So if you continue to bring them value, they will gladly reciprocate it. Also, by becoming a useful to them, word will get around. Then you'll have a line of influential people eager to work with you.

Conclusion

Who you spend the most time with will determine your results. And there is no better group who will help you multiply your results quicker and in a greater way than your center of influence network.

If you want to 100X your results, you need to spend time with the kind of people who are already getting those results. 100X your network by adding the most influential people you can find to it and then bring them great value. By doing this, they will gladly reciprocate through the advice they give, the opportunities they share and the other influential people they introduce you to.

How do you do this?

Make it a routine to spend time with 10X more influencers weekly, and then dedicate yourself to bringing them 10X more value. This way you will 100X your network and then 100X your business results. Because 10X times 10X equals 100X!

Now that you have learned how to create a powerful peer group that will greatly multiply your efforts, it's time to learn how to leverage all the money that these influential people will help you make.

So if you want to learn how to take every $1 you make, and multiply by 100X, then turn the page because that is the subject of our next chapter.

ACTION STEPS

1. Block out time in your weekly schedule to commit to consistently meeting with influential people.
2. Begin contacting them to set-up times to meet.
3. Bring them abundant value and show your appreciation by meeting their needs.
4. At your meetings, also ask them to introduce you to other influential people they know.

Pitfalls to Avoid

1. Not all influential people are created equal. Therefore, build relationships with those with similar values to yours and who don't violate your beliefs.

100X YOUR FINANCES

"In the entrepreneurial world, it's not about resources, but about being resourceful."
– Chris Gardner

Brian Chesky was born on August 29, 1981, in Niskayuna, New York. His early life was marked by a creative streak, with a keen interest in art and design. He attended the Rhode Island School of Design (RISD) where he met Joe Gebbia, who would later become his business partner.

After graduation, Chesky moved to Los Angeles to work as an industrial designer. However, in 2007, facing financial struggles, he moved to San Francisco to live with Gebbia.

In October 2007, Chesky and Gebbia were struggling to pay rent. Spotting an opportunity, they decided to rent out air mattresses in their living room after finding out that a design conference in San

Francisco had led to a shortage of hotel rooms. This idea gave birth to "Airbed and Breakfast"—later known as "Airbnb."

They created a simple website, offering guests breakfast and a place to sleep. This initial start was not just a financial necessity but also proof of concept for what would become a global phenomenon.

Chesky's frugality and resourcefulness was evident in the early days of Airbnb. The founders didn't have the capital to compete with large hotel chains or fund massive marketing campaigns. Instead, they focused on creating a unique, personal experience for guests. They personally photographed the listings to ensure quality and authenticity, a practice that later evolved into a professional photography program for Airbnb hosts.

These early examples of resourcefulness and frugality were crucial in Airbnb's survival and growth. Airbnb thrived by offering affordable lodging options—even though the 2008 financial crisis presented a challenging economic environment. Chesky's focus on community building, trust between hosts and guests, and leveraging technology for ease of use, were pivotal in Airbnb's scalability and success.

Over the years, Chesky's frugal and resourceful approach steered Airbnb through various challenges, including regulatory hurdles and the COVID-19 pandemic. His ability to adapt, focus on core values, and maintain a user-centric approach not only helped Airbnb survive but also thrive.

Chesky's journey is a remarkable story of how innovative thinking, coupled with frugality and resourcefulness, can revolutionize an industry, and change how people travel and connect.

Boom or Bust

Brian Chesky is another great example of an entrepreneur who didn't start his business with much. But he turned a losing situation into a billion-dollar company through his resourcefulness, frugality, creativity, and determination. He not only disrupted the global hotel industry, but revolutionized travel around the world.

By using nimble and resourceful hacks, and a lot of duct-tape, he controlled his costs and continued to create massive value for customers.

This gives us a glimpse of what an entrepreneur must do to handle the finances of his or her business effectively, while building a successful enterprise at the same time.

Finances, or the lack thereof, have been cited as one of the greatest causes of business failure in every business industry in history. Entrepreneurs usually don't have enough money to start, so they aren't able to market, hire new people, or support themselves while the business takes flight. Or their lack of money means they must do all the work themselves, working themselves to the bone, and eventually running out of steam.

Some entrepreneurs start with a lot of money, but it slowly erodes because of unwise financial decisions, resulting in not giving them enough time to bring a valuable product to market. And in some cases, your competitor has a lot more money than you, so they outspend you and you never seem to be able to catch up.

From Brian Chesky's example, we can learn that with the right attitude, a budding entrepreneur can not only dominate, but can 100X+ their business results as well.

Start With Character

The three characteristics that Brian Chesky demonstrated through his bumpy entrepreneurial career, and which ultimately helped him survive and thrive through it, are: **frugality**, **resourcefulness**, and **creativity.**

Frugality

Frugality is defined as the wise use of our resources. It doesn't mean being cheap. On the contrary, frugal individuals do spend money, but they spend it in a way they know they will get a substantial return for each dollar they spend.

The HBO documentary, "Being Warren Buffet," follows a day in the life of Warren Buffett, and an instance when he stopped at a McDonald's to grab a meal. As he paid for his order, he meticulously counted out the exact change, $3.17, down to the last penny.

In another interview, when asked why he does this (a habit he's been doing for the past five decades), Buffett, with a twinkle in his eye, offered a profound insight. He explained that the dollar he just spent was not merely a dollar in his eyes. That dollar represents much more in the world of investing, where money has the potential to grow exponentially. He believed that every dollar wasted was not just a dollar lost but potentially a million dollars not earned.

For Buffett, it wasn't about the value of money at that moment, but its potential future value.

Frugality is **seeing every dollar, not as a dollar, but as the million dollars it could be in the future.** Seeing money this way changes the value each dollar has to us, making it a whole lot harder to waste.

This way of thinking causes you to see expenses differently also. Now, every expense is no longer seen as an expense but as an investment. And every expense now requires a return. Therefore, frugality means not spending money unless there is a justifiable reason and a high return coming from it.

Reflection Checkpoint

1. What are your three biggest expenses?
2. What kind of return are you getting for these expenses?
3. What can you do to increase the return on your investment?

This is very different than how some entrepreneurs spend money in business. For example, many entrepreneurs spend money on marketing, even though a lot of times there is no justifiable return. Then they throw even more money into it, hoping for a return, but instead, not only does it fail to give a return, but you end up losing all your money. Then we proceed to throw even more money into it.

Who in their right mind does that?

I say this because this was how I operated my business when I first started my entrepreneurial journey. And not surprisingly, my business crashed and burned.

Yet, it taught me a lesson I will never forget. After this experience, I decided that I would never spend money unnecessarily on marketing. I would make sure I was getting a return first, and only then would I spend money on marketing.

One way I did this was by getting my marketing done for free. For example, one time I contacted a marketing company and made a deal with them. I promised I would bring them five customers in exchange for free marketing services. For them, it was a no-brainer, so that is what I did. I found five customers for them, and then I got my marketing for free.

Another time, I found a SEO company and negotiated their rates down to as low as I could get it. Then I resold their services to my clients at a premium, and used the profit to pay for my marketing also. The key principle to learn from both Brian Chesky and Warren Buffet is that every dollar you spend is important, and so it requires a return. In other words, just spending money to spend it is unacceptable. Rather, you need to find other, less expensive, and resourceful ways to get what you need, so that you can conserve your cash, make it last longer, and get a great return from it.

Resourcefulness

A television show called MacGyver premiered on September 29, 1985. The show's protagonist, Angus MacGyver, became a legend for his resourceful ability to use everyday materials to resolve dangerous situations, often with little more than duct tape, a paperclip, and a Swiss Army knife.

Resourcefulness is the ability to find quick and clever ways to overcome difficulties. It is thinking "out of the box" to find solutions to overcome the everyday challenges that come your way.

In business, the most common challenges you will face are financially-related. Difficulties such as:

- Finding money to start your business.
- Finding ways to pay for your business needs when revenue is low.
- Searching for financing to grow your business.
- Facing economic downturns that can drastically reduce your revenue.

While many entrepreneurs are floored by these challenges, like MacGyver, resourceful entrepreneurs will use everything at their disposal to overcome their situation.

For example, one of the most resourceful efforts by Chesky and his team was the "Obama O's" and "Cap'n McCains" cereal boxes campaign during the 2008 U.S. presidential election. They designed and produced two limited-edition cereal boxes: "Obama O's: The Breakfast of Change" and "Cap'n McCains: A Maverick in Every Bite." These regular rebranded cereal boxes with caricatures and slogans reflected the presidential candidates Barack Obama and John McCain. The idea was to create a buzz and capitalize on the election fever that gripped the nation.

The team initially handmade about 500 boxes, selling them for $40 each. It demonstrated Chesky and his team's ability to think resourcefully and leverage current events to generate interest and publicity. The campaign was a surprising success, helping them raise $30,000.

Creativity

Creativity (in business) is defined as the tendency to generate or recognize ideas, alternatives, or possibilities that might be useful in solving problems and communicating with others.

Creativity is especially useful in entrepreneurship because sometimes the obvious solution to a difficult problem isn't always readily available. Or the obstacles can totally shipwreck an endeavor, leaving you wondering what you'll do with the left-over pieces.

Many entrepreneurs will sometimes just give up and throw in the towel. But the creative entrepreneur will find a new way, a new possibility, or take advantage of the new opportunities open to them and create an even better outcome.

This attitude was the catalyst that sparked the idea of Airbnb. When Chesky and Gebbia were struggling to pay rent, they decided to get creative and rented out air mattresses in their living room. They set-up a simple website, advertising a place to stay with the bonus of a home-cooked breakfast. This initiative was initially meant to be a temporary solution to their immediate financial problems. But as we know, the rest is history.

What would you have done in that situation? Maybe ask a relative for money? Or maybe just throw in the towel and move to a more affordable city? If Chesky had done that, there would be no Airbnb today. Instead, Chesky decided he would tap into his creative side, and took up the opportunity that was presented to him.

I also faced a similar situation in December 2014 when I couldn't pay rent, and I had limited options. I had other options, such as moving in with my in-laws, or moving to another less expensive city.

But instead, I stopped and asked myself the question, **"What opportunities does this situation open up for me?"**

That question jumpstarted my creative juices, and I developed the Passive Income webinar, whose success was the beginning of all the financial success I have today. If I hadn't paused and let my creativity kick in, I doubt I would even be writing this book today.

End with Strategy

Now that we've discussed the character it takes to dominate the financial challenges that entrepreneurship will bring, let's talk about the strategy that will help you multiply your financial returns.

The financial results we are looking for isn't just about learning how to do effective bookkeeping; rather, we want to turn every $1 to $10, or even $100, of value.

Get 10X from Every Dollar You Spend

If you want to get more value for every dollar you spend, first begin practicing allocating your money in ways that will give you a 10X return or more. This means that you will no longer be satisfied just getting $1 worth of value for every $1 you spend. No, you want to get $10 or $100 worth of value for each $1, and even better if we can get that for every .10 cents.

To do this, it takes frugality, resourcefulness, creativity, and flexibility to operate differently than every other entrepreneur operates.

Brian Chesky's effort at transforming a $2 pack of bulk generic cereal into a $40 box of Obama O's is a great example.

I also experienced this in my children's publishing company. The eBooks had already been written and I was making a set amount of money from them. Then I thought, **"How can I get 10X the amount of revenue and profits for these books?"** That sparked the idea of offering a paperback version, a hardback version, and an audio version. I even shopped around to see if I could get a movie made from them as well.

That greatly multiplied our returns, but then I again thought, **"How can I 10X the returns even more?"** So that's when I came up with the idea of licensing my books globally and supplying them to libraries and other bookstores around the world. The best part was that all I needed to do was post my books in certain distribution houses. This way, the work needed to get my book to bookstores around the world was done automatically for me.

So imagine, I made the books once, and then I multiplied the returns by finding multiple creative ways to distribute the books in different formats, languages, and locations and generate 10X more money.

Here is a list of ideas you can use to multiply the return on every dollar you spend in your business:

1. **Upsells and Cross-sells:** Create new high-value products and sell them for top dollar to as many of your current customers as possible.
2. **Automated Accounts Receivable:** Use software to automate invoicing and follow-ups, ensuring faster payments and improved cash flow.
3. **Monetize Excess Capacity:** If you have unused space or resources, rent them out or offer them as a service.
4. **Dynamic Pricing:** Use dynamic pricing strategies to adjust prices based on demand, maximizing revenue.
5. **Implement Value-Based Pricing:** Charge based on the value provided to customers rather than just cost-plus pricing.
6. **Subscription Model:** If applicable, switch to a subscription-based revenue model for predictable, recurring income.
7. **Offer Subscription Upgrades:** Provide premium subscription options with added features for a higher price.
8. **Loyalty Programs:** Create loyalty programs to increase customer retention and lifetime value.
9. **Offer Bundled Services:** Increase average order value by bundling products or services together at a discounted rate.
10. **Joint Ventures:** Enter into joint ventures to share costs and risks while accessing new markets or technologies.

*For hundreds more ideas on how to increase your revenue by 10X, ask the 100X AI Business Advisor for FREE here: 100xbusinessadvisor.ai.

The key to multiplying your returns by 10X is to stack as many of these revenue-multiplying strategies as possible. The combined result will multiply your returns by 10X or even 100X for each dollar you spend.

Reduce Your Expenses by 10X

Getting $10 worth of value for each $1 is good. But do you know what is better? Getting $10 worth of value for each .10 cents.

Multiply your returns substantially by reducing your expenses by 10X. This not only reduces the amount you are putting at risk, but it will also increase your profits at the same time.

The key is to try to get the value you need for free, if possible, or close to it, by reducing the amount of time, effort, and resources you put out. I know this sounds hard to believe, but the number of opportunities to get resources for free are so abundant in the world today that I would be remiss if I did not mention them.

For example, Brian Chesky's Obama O's strategy didn't only generate funds for their startup. At the time, they were having a difficult time finding investors for their business. This was a clever marketing strategy to get free publicity by leveraging current events and generating public interest. The success of the campaign helped Airbnb get the attention they needed, which eventually led to their acceptance into Y Combinator, a startup accelerator program.

The good news is that reducing expenses is the fastest way to make money in a business. If you are creative enough, you can unlock thousands of dollars by just finding creative ways to get the resources you need for free, or using less time, effort, resources, and money (TERM).

For example, for my publishing company, I personally wrote the first 18 books in the kid's book series. To reduce my time, effort, and resources, I contracted a ghost writer to write the next books for me. I continued to make money on the new books we were publishing, and I didn't even have to write them anymore. And, at the time of this writing, we have 46 books in the series—most of which I didn't even have to write.

Here is a list of ways you can quickly reduce the TERM your business expends, that combined, will greatly reduce your expenses by 10X:

1. **Remote Work:** Go completely remote to save office space and utilities.
2. **Negotiate Rent:** Renegotiate rent or move to a less expensive location.
3. **Negotiate with Vendors:** Renegotiate with all vendor contracts to reduce costs, but still bring benefit to your vendor and business.
4. **Outsourcing:** Outsource tasks to lower-cost providers.
5. **Video Conferencing:** Use video conferencing to cut down on travel expenses.
6. **Automation:** Automate processes with software to reduce labor costs.
7. **Consolidation:** Consolidate software subscriptions and eliminate redundant tools.
8. **Cloud Services:** Use cloud services to reduce IT infrastructure and maintenance costs.

9. **Bulk Purchasing:** Implement bulk buying and negotiate volume discounts with suppliers.
10. **Cross Training:** Cross-train employees to cover multiple roles.

*For hundreds more ideas on how to reduce your expenses by 10X, ask the 100X AI Business Advisor for FREE here: 100xbusinessadvisor.ai.

Reflection Checkpoint

1. What are some creative ways you can reduce your current expenses without sacrificing the quality of your product or service?
2. How quickly can you make these changes?

The 20% Rule

The 20% Rule is a very effective system to help you 10X the return on each dollar you spend and reduce your expenses by 10X. The 20% rule is a strategy that dictates that, every month or quarter, you devote the time to creatively increase the return on each dollar by 20% and reduce your expenses by 20%.

The strategy can be implemented by scheduling 3–4 hours each month or quarter for you and your team to attack the budget with creative ideas to both increase value and reduce expenses. Go after the larger expenses first because a 20% haircut off a large expense will lead to substantial savings. Then stair-step to the smallest expenses.

Be as creative as you need to be and come up with the most hair-brained ideas you can. The key is to brainstorm and think outside the box.

Use the strategies in this chapter and see if any can be implemented to give you the quickest increase in value and decrease in expense. The more ideas you use, the greater the cumulative impact.

Consistency is the key to the success of this strategy. You will operate leaner if you consistently meet every month or every quarter to brainstorm how to shave away expenses and increase value. And you will get closer and closer to making sure that each $1 spent in the business brings $10, or even $100, worth of value.

Conclusion

There is no greater challenge in business than allocating finances in a way that keeps you constantly in the black. But with an attitude of frugality, resourcefulness, and creativity, you'll be able to weather any storm and even identify new game-changing opportunities from them.

The key to 100X your finances will be to increase the value of each dollar you spend by 10X while reducing your expenses by 10X. You can achieve this by consistently attacking your finances every month or quarter with your team, and brainstorming ways to increase your value and lower expenses. And before you know it, you will be getting 100X more value for each dollar you spend.

Now it's time to learn how to get mind boggling returns for all your efforts that far exceed 100X. If you are ready to go supersonic in your results, then just turn the page because that is the subject of our next chapter.

ACTION STEPS

1. Set-up a 3–4 hour financial brainstorm meeting with your team.
2. Give them a copy of the budget, and list all your expense items from largest to smallest.
3. Using the list of ideas in this chapter, come up with ways to decrease expenses in the organization by 20.Start with higher cost items first.
4. Schedule a time to do this each month or quarter.

Pitfalls to Avoid

1. Do not reduce the expense of an item if it will result in reducing the quality or value you bring to your customers, team, or the business overall.

100X

100X YOUR OPPORTUNITIES

"Business opportunities are like buses, there's always another one coming."
– Richard Branson

Born on January 29, 1954, in Kosciusko, Mississippi, Oprah Gail Winfrey's early life was far from the glitz and glamour she is associated with today. Her childhood was steeped in poverty and marked by significant challenges, including being raised in a low-income household and experiencing abuse and hardship.

Oprah's life on her grandmother's farm in Mississippi was her first exposure to poverty. Despite the struggles, this period also planted the seeds of her love for books and learning, a passion that would later become a cornerstone of her career. Her grandmother was a significant influence and encouraged her to read and speak in public, laying the foundation for her future endeavors.

The turning point in Oprah's life came with a scholarship to Tennessee State University where she studied communications. Her innate talent for speaking and connecting with people led her to the media industry, where she first dipped her toes in radio broadcasting.

A pivotal moment in Oprah's career came when a local radio station, WVOL, needed someone to fill in for an absent newsreader. Oprah seized this unexpected opportunity, delivering an impromptu news reading performance that impressed the station managers. Recognizing her talent and potential, they offered her a job as a radio news anchor on the spot.

Then in 1973, at the age of 19, Oprah Winfrey took a significant step in her career by becoming the youngest and first African American female news anchor at Nashville's WLAC-TV (now WTVF), a CBS affiliate. This opportunity was groundbreaking, not only for Oprah personally but also in the context of the media landscape at the time, which was pre-dominantly white males.

The transition from news to talk shows was another pivotal moment in Oprah's career. Her empathetic, personal style was better suited to the talk show format. This shift occurred when she moved to Baltimore's WJZ-TV in 1976 to co-host the talk show "People Are Talking." Here, Oprah truly began to flourish. The show's success was largely attributed to her warm, approachable demeanor and her ability to connect with both her guests and the audience.

Then, in 1984, she relocated to Chicago to host WLS-TV's low-rated half-hour morning talk show, "AM Chicago." In September 1986, the show was subsequently renamed "The Oprah Winfrey Show," expanded to a full hour, and broadcasted nationally.

Because of Oprah's warm, engaging style and her ability to connect with her audience, the show quickly rose to dominate talk show ratings. This groundbreaking talk show ran for 25 years and became a cultural phenomenon, cementing Oprah's status as a media powerhouse.

Oprah's early opportunities in radio news broadcasting was the launchpad that propelled her into a career that would eventually redefine American talk shows and media in general. It showcased her unique abilities and set the stage for her to become a powerful, influential figure in television and beyond.

The Secret of Success

In the book, "Outliers," Malcolm Gladwell argues that success is not just about individual achievement, but it's also shaped by aspects such as timing, opportunities, cultural background, and the support people receive along the way.

In other words, you can achieve a lot if you're talented. But with the right timing, environment, and opportunities, you can have a substantially greater impact.

Gladwell uses examples of how Bill Gates, Steve Jobs, and Paul Allen had an accelerated path toward success because they were the ideal age (their hyper 20s), had early access to special technology (access to early computer models), in the perfect location (tech hubs like

Silicon Valley and Seattle), and in the perfect environment (the computing revolution era) to make it big. (You can see a similar trend play out in the 2000s with Mark Zuckerberg, Sergey Brin, Larry Page, Jeff Bezos, and Elon Musk).

Though Oprah Winfrey's background created many obstacles to her success, a few opportunities early in life, such as being accepted to Tennessee State University, and the serendipitous opportunity to substitute for an absent radio news anchor, provided her with the springboard she needed to showcase her talents and ultimately put her on track to becoming the media mogul she is today.

In this book, we've already discussed how chance opportunities played a huge role in the meteoric rise of many successful entrepreneurs. Sarah Blakely's skyrocketing success with Spanx came after a chance mention by Oprah Winfrey in her list of favorite products in 2000. Daymond John's FUBU label quickly surged to the national stage after his childhood friend, LL Cool J, was offered the chance to do a national commercial for the Gap. Even a fledgling, unpopular messaging app named WhatsApp, suddenly experienced blazing success due to an unforeseen change in the App Store algorithm that now allowed for push notifications.

History is littered with chance opportunities that became the pivotal turning points for some of the most successful people and businesses we know today. Here are a few other examples you may recognize:

1. **Steve Jobs and Steve Wozniak (Apple):** Met through a mutual high school friend who introduced them when he heard they both liked electronics.

2. **Larry Page and Sergey Brin (Google):** Met by chance at Stanford University when Brin was assigned to show Page around.

3. **Mark Zuckerberg and Sean Parker:** Zuckerberg's chance meeting with Napster co-founder Sean Parker at a party helped pivot Facebook's strategy and secure funding.

4. **Travis Kalanick and Garrett Camp (Uber):** Uber was born from a chance conversation between Kalanick and Camp during a shared cab ride in Paris after a tech conference.

5. **Jan Koum and Brian Acton (WhatsApp):** Both former employees of Yahoo met during an audit and later started WhatsApp.

6. **Bill Hewlett and Dave Packard (Hewlett-Packard):** They met through a friend at Stanford University, leading to the creation of HP in a garage.

7. **Caterina Fake and Stewart Butterfield (Flickr):** Met at an educational conference and later co-founded Flickr.

8. **Herb Kelleher and Rollin King (Southwest Airlines):** Met by chance and doodled the concept of Southwest Airlines on a napkin.

9. **Ben Silbermann and Paul Sciarra (Pinterest):** Met at a New York City reception and later co-founded Pinterest.

10. **Martin Eberhard and Marc Tarpenning (Tesla Motors):** Met during a social event and later founded Tesla Motors.

These chance encounters led to opportunities that allowed them not just to be more successful than others, but 100X+ more successful.

What's the principle that we can learn from these examples? That if you want to be successful, having great talent and character will get you far. But if you want to attain 100X, 1000X and even 10,000X greater returns, you'll need to tap into the magic of exponential opportunities.

The Magic of Exponential Opportunities

Exponential opportunities are rare, random, yet powerful opportunities that fall into your lap when you least expect it. They are so impactful that they can catapult you and your profits to a mind boggling level. They come without warning and disappear without a trace. But if you are lucky enough to be prepared when it comes, the rewards are jaw-dropping.

The challenge is that only a few people stumble onto these chance opportunities, and no matter how much they try, they can't replicate the outcome. These are the "one-hit wonders" that eventually fade from our memories over time.

So how can you position yourself to capture a significant amount of these opportunities, and 100X your returns, whenever and however you want?

The one pattern that is consistent among many of these examples of successful people is that they were in a certain place and time that led to the perfect opportunity that was the springboard to their success. Like Gladwell said, exponential opportunities are created when the timing, environment, strategy, team, and training is ideal.

The fact is that opportunities are environment-dependent. Being in certain environments with a history of success increases the chances you will experience those opportunities as well. This was the argument put forth in a Forbes article by Matt Durot entitled "More Than One-Fourth of America's 400 Richest Went To One Of These 12 Colleges."

This article states that among the Forbes 400, 71 billionaires went to Ivy League institutions such as Harvard, the University of Pennsylvania, and Yale. Harvard University tops the list with the most alumni on The Forbes 400. The University of Pennsylvania and Yale University also featured prominently on this list.

In other words, **positioning yourself in environments known to attract greater opportunities will increase your chances of accessing those opportunities.**

Putting Yourself in a Winning Position

> "Opportunity dances with those who are already on the dance floor."
> **– H. Jackson Brown Jr.**

Let's take a look at a list of successful environments that can give you the highest chance of finding opportunities that will 100X your results.

Successful People

As we've discussed throughout this book, spending time with successful people will increase your chances of finding more exponential opportunities. This is because successful people are highly influential, and can use that influence to help you as well.

Successful people can:

- Refer business to you that could **open doors** that you would not have had access to otherwise.
- **Challenge your thinking**, and help you see the opportunities in front of you that you are currently missing.
- **Introduce** you to other successful people, which will open even more chances to find great opportunities.

In other words, because success attracts success, the more time you spend with successful people, the better your chances of some of those opportunities dropping into your lap.

Successful Places

The reality is that historically, some places just have a whole lot more success stories than others (Think Silicon Valley vs Topeka, Kansas). Durot's Forbes article supported this idea by showing how over one-fourth of America's richest people attended one of twelve universities.

The idea, therefore, is that if you spend more time where the most success stories come from, you'll have a greater chance of being one of those success stories. Therefore, if you want to be successful, you probably want to live and work in whatever cities that have the most millionaires, multi-millionaires, and billionaires.

Now, Ivy league universities and metropolitan cities aren't the only places you can find successful people. You can also find them at events, such as business and tech conferences, non-profit charity galas, high-level social gatherings, and business-themed educational events. Many of the success stories listed in this chapter met at many of these types of gatherings.

Successful Groups

Being part of the right group will also give you access to a lot of unique opportunities exclusive to only a few. The good news is that many of these groups are accessible to anyone for a fee.

Business networks and mastermind groups are a great source that will give you exposure to successful people, or those who will be successful in the future. Also becoming part of a business's board of directors or board of advisors can expose you to many other successful people and opportunities as well.

Now some of these groups usually charge a fee, so my advice is to do everything in your power to scrape all you can to pay for the membership because the return you get will easily 100X your initial investment.

In my early foray into entrepreneurship, I joined a group called Maui Mastermind, which I would say had the greatest influence on my life and business career to this day. Many of the things I learned were timeless business principles that are still the foundation of the way I do business today. Now, the entrance fee to this group wasn't cheap (and I am glad it wasn't). But with confidence, I can say that I have made 100X my return from all the lessons, contacts, and opportunities I received.

Another source where you can find high-level opportunities is joining non-profit boards or their organizations. You can usually find highly successful people there who have big hearts to give back to the community. By coming together for quarterly meetings, you would be surprised how many highly influential people you meet and can quickly connect with because of your affiliation.

Successful Timing

Finding the hottest and most in-demand trends and building relevant, timely solutions that will meet the demand will create exponential opportunities that bring outsized results. Jumping on a current hot trend with a valuable solution will take any success you have and multiply it astronomically. Some popular trends over time include computers in the 80s, the internet in the 90s, social media in the 2000s, and now AI in the 2020s. Many of the world's most successful billionaires have a history of either creating market trends through innovative products and services or recognizing and investing in emerging trends before they become mainstream. Examples include technology trends such as the internet, e-commerce, and social media, mobile phones, renewable energy, electric vehicles, and biotechnology.

Many entrepreneurs fall into the trap of believing that because many entrepreneurs are jumping on a trend then the market is over-saturated. This couldn't be further from the truth. They are mostly encountering news from innovators and early adopters because this is mostly what entrepreneurs read about. Yet, usually, there are billions of people who are clueless to the new market trends because they are usually more risk-averse and will wait for years before jumping on a trend. This leaves a lot of room for entrepreneurs to jump into the fray and create some magic of their own.

For example, as of writing this book, artificial intelligence (AI) is the new major trend in the world today (mostly among innovators and early adopters). Yet, if I were to ask a random stranger in the middle of Nebraska what AI is, they would look at me like I have three heads. This is because it hasn't yet become the norm for the mainstream public leaving a lot of room to create all different kinds of products and services for when the mainstream catches on.

Successful Teams

Trying to achieve success working alone is possible, but rare. This is because working alone will keep you isolated and limited. On the other hand, building powerful teams with other successful people will open new resources, new talents, bigger networks, and greater possibilities you wouldn't be able to get on your own.

The synergy created by being part of a powerful team will take a 2X, 3X and even 10X return, and easily turn it into 100X. This makes finding powerful teams a great catalyst to success, and why so many startups try their best to get into some of the best business incubators or accelerators with the best track records of success.

The good news is that if you can't get into one of the most popular startup incubators and accelerators, there are many more groups of scrappy, hungry startup groups and meetups that can serve the same purpose. They will probably cost a fee, but it will be one of the wisest investments you can ever make. And it will give you the greatest chance of attracting opportunities that can 100X your results.

And if you get the idea in your head that you can become successful by working alone, consider that almost 100% of successful people in history have worked with a team.

Conclusion

Talent and character alone can make you successful. But when you add exponential opportunities to the mix, you create the potential for returns of 100X and beyond. However, since exponential opportunities are usually random, finding them is not easy.

It takes putting yourself in the kind of successful environments that attract as many of those opportunities as possible.

Here are a few takeaways:

- **Surrounding yourself with successful people** will enable you to not only be influenced by them but also receive benefits when they share their opportunities with you.
- Visiting places that have **a history of success stories** will also increase your chances of becoming one.
- Being **part of successful groups** increases your chance of encounters with people and opportunities that can change your future.
- Hitching a ride on **a popular trend** will give you the momentum you need to boost your success to astronomical levels.
- Being **part of groups of successful teams** working toward a goal will enhance your chances of seeing more exponential opportunities in your lifetime.By putting yourself in these successful environments, you won't just have 2X, 3X or even

10X results, you will 100X your results, catapulting you and your business toward infinity and beyond.

ACTION STEPS

1. **Successful People:** Make an appointment with 2–3 successful people every week. Eventually raise it to 5–6 a week.
2. **Successful Places:** Visit 1–2 business conferences a month frequented by successful people.
3. **Successful Groups:** Set aside money to invest in being part of the business group of an entrepreneur you admire and join it today.
4. **Successful Timing:** Consider the latest trends, and build products and services based on those trends that fill gaps in the market that you care about.
5. **Successful Teams:** Fill out an application to be part of some famous business incubators and accelerators. If you get rejected, at least they know who you are. Then join smaller local incubators and do some noteworthy things that can get you noticed by the more famous ones.

Pitfalls to Avoid

1. Don't go after every opportunity. Make sure whatever opportunity you go after aligns with your values, guidelines, and long-term goals.
2. The same goes for the successful people you meet. Make sure that the people you meet have comparable values and goals and stay away from those that violate them.

CONCLUSION

It has been an exciting journey learning about how to generate 100X results in your life and business.

In this conclusion, we will take some time to summarize all that we've learned. After you finish this book, this conclusion can serve as an overview of the key learning points. So, instead of re-reading this book, going forward, you can use this summary as a quick refresher of the key 100X principles we've talked about. You can also use it as a reference guide as you apply these principles daily in your business and life.

Part 1—The Foundation

We started our discussion in Part 1 by defining 100X and discussing the foundational principles behind this powerful philosophy.

What is 100X?

100X

100X is the idea that you can operate in a way to get 10X greater results using 10X less time, effort, resources, and money (TERM). It is similar to the philosophy of 10X, by Grant Cardone, except, instead of using massive action to get 10X results—which might be unsustainable over the long run—you can work smarter by using massive leverage.

100X works because it is an extension of powerful universal principles that drive you forward with little effort. The main universal principles driving 100X are the 80/20 principle, Parkinson's law, Occam's Razor, Kaizen, and First Principles Thinking.

There are powerful elements in the universe, that, though small, have a massive and profound impact on this world. They are all around us in science, nature, technology, relationships and more. These forces are the source behind the power of 100X. Yet, these forces are missed by many, even though they are in plain sight. So it takes courage and effort to seek and harness these forces. And by imitating the many courageous entrepreneurs of the past, you can seek and find these drivers, and direct their power toward creating 100X results in your life and business.

Part 2—100X Yourself

Part 2 focused on how to apply these 100X principles in your life. There is no greater catalyst to growing your business than growing yourself. You will quickly achieve the 100X results you are looking for if you apply these 100X principles to growing your life first.

Like the saying goes, "If you want to grow your business, you need to grow yourself."

We all have limits we put on ourselves. The way to overcome those limits is by shifting to a 100X mindset. We do this by first multiplying our goals by 10X because this helps to quickly blow away your mental limits and triggers us to identify the highest priorities necessary to reach those goals. Then, we can go after our goals substantially faster by deciding to accomplish our tasks in 10X less time. We can radically speed up the process to our success by reducing the time we give ourselves to accomplish our projects from years to months, or from months to weeks or days.

You can 100X your character by getting rid of the head trash that's holding you back. You can attack the limiting beliefs that are the foundation of your head trash by using the 4 Truth questions, and quickly invalidate them. And further, speed up your internal growth through the power of visualization. Lastly, you can achieve your goals faster by saturating your environment with other 100X individuals, who will have such a powerful influence on our lives that ultimately, we will become more like them over time.

Focus is another essential key to success. Yet with the 10,000 things we must do in business, figuring out what is most important can be challenging. Yet, we can quickly identify what is most valuable by learning to 100X our focus. We do this by first applying a dollar figure to all our tasks, which will clarify what is most valuable. Then we can shave off our schedule any tasks that are not valuable by using a stop doing list, until only the highest value tasks remain.

We also learned how to be 100X more productive by identifying the Magic 1% tasks that bring the greatest impact to our business. By devoting ourselves to ONLY doing these tasks, we will be able to consistently generate 100X results like the uber successful people we admire. We can also ensure we do these high-value tasks consistently by putting them on our schedule and committing daily to doing these tasks first.

Last, the strategy you use is also highly essential and critical to success. We learned we need to focus on a 3-Level approach to success to 100X our strategy. The three levels are: the Incremental, Exponential and Explosive growth levels of success.

The Incremental growth level produces incremental gains over a long period of time. Though valuable, they need to be delegated because the tasks are repetitive and the results come incrementally. We need to spend 80% of our time and effort on the Exponential Growth level because it brings rapid large-scale results. We also need to dedicate ourselves to the Explosive Growth level, by putting ourselves in the right environments to attract more explosive opportunities and 100X our results.

Part 3—100X Your Business

Part 3 discussed taking the 100X principles and applying them to each section of your business.

Historically, business ideas have a high rate of failure. Yet, you can substantially increase your chance of success if you 100X your business ideas. You can do this by first making sure that your ideas bring 10X more value than your competitors by either being 10X less expensive or 10X easier to use. Then you want to deliver that value to customers using 10X less TERM. This way, 10X more value, using 10X less TERM, will bring you a 100X greater chance of success.

You need to have a strong competitive advantage to get an edge in business. Iron-clad competitive advantages that offer legal protection are critical to protecting your ideas from being copied. When those aren't accessible, stacking dynamic advantages, which you can create yourself, can give you the edge you need to dominate the marketplace. By stacking many levels of these advantages, you'll be able to build such a lead over your competitors that you can gain the lion's share of the market and make it, so they never catch up.

To 100X your marketing returns, you need to focus on a 3-Level marketing approach. You can increase the likelihood of a quicker, rapid scale impact from your marketing efforts by focusing 80% of your attention on the exponential and explosive marketing efforts, and delegating, automating, and simplifying your incremental efforts.

You can create these exponential jumps in your marketing by building relationships with influencers who will spread your message to thousands of people. Also, by putting yourself in environments to attract explosive opportunities, you will increase your chance of taking advantage of these opportunities and taking your business to mind boggling levels. Last, by spending 20% of your time using low-cost, short-term incremental marketing efforts, you can continue to build incremental gains, establishing a strong, long-term foundation for years to come.

Successful sales, though elusive, are the greatest determining factor for your business success. Yet, by focusing your efforts on providing 10X more value for customers and reducing 10X the risk for customers in making their purchases, you will create the type of irresistible offers that will guarantee the sale. Also, by focusing on the ideal superfan customers, and even targeting the higher end of the market, you will create so much value that not only will the sale be a forgone conclusion, but you can also expect 100X the return for all your sales efforts.

The system you use to operate your business is also an integral part of fulfilling the promises you make to customers. Because of fierce competition in the marketplace, one of the greatest ways to get an edge in business is to operate in the leanest way possible without affecting the quality you bring to customers. Use First Principles thinking to shave away 10X more unnecessary steps in your operations. Also, by adding simple steps that create 10X more value, you'll be able to have the best of both worlds, and 100X your revenues and profits, while creating very happy customers.

Your peer group will determine the level of success you will have as a leader and business. Making the effort to 100X your network by surrounding yourself with high-value individuals can create a massive jump in your results. These individuals challenge your thinking, boldly call you out on your excuses, open doors to new opportunities, and introduce you to other influential people. Therefore meeting with 10X more of these individuals monthly and bringing them 10X more value will create the perfect storm to multiply your results by 100X.

The ability to effectively allocate your finances will give you a substantial edge in your business. This requires an attitude of frugality, resourcefulness, and creativity that will help you stay in the black, as well as weather any financial storm that may come. The key strategy to 100X your finances will be to increase the value of each dollar you spend by 10X while reducing your expenses by 10X. Consistently brainstorming ways to increase your value and lower expenses will provide you with 100X more value for each dollar that you spend.

The right opportunity can quickly 100X your results and change your life and business in an unprecedented way. Positioning yourself in successful environments will greatly increase your chances of attracting opportunities that can 100X your results.

This can include surrounding yourself with successful people who share their opportunities with you, visiting places that have a history of success stories, and being part of successful groups that increases your chance of encounters with people and opportunities who can change your future. Also, hitching a ride on a popular trend will give you the momentum that can boost your chances of encountering a great opportunity. Last, being part of groups of successful teams who are working toward a goal will create synergy that will enhance your chances of landing abundant, highly lucrative opportunities in your entrepreneurial career.

Conclusion

Now the time has come to say farewell. I hand the torch over to you to take the next step and begin implementing these principles in your life and business. These principles are incredibly powerful and have brought me, and the many successful entrepreneur examples in this book, 100X results and more. But like a car with 400 horsepower that just sits in your garage, these principles will be useless to you until you decide to push the gas and take it out for a ride by applying them yourself.

If I, and the many other successful entrepreneurs in this book can do it, so can you. Therefore, I wish you the best of luck in your entrepreneurial journey.

And again, if you need support, like most of us do, please join our 100X Entrepreneur's Club to receive more inspirational emails on how to practically apply 100X.

Here is the link:

https://www.100xbusinessadvisor.com/100xbookclub

To your success!

Will Peña 2024
Weston, Florida

100X YOUR RESULTS WITH THE POWER OF AI

So what is 100X in a nutshell?

The principle of 100X, in its simplest form, concerns not only spending time thinking about "what" to do but spending time thinking about the "way" to do things.

100X is really all about taking a pause.

The Space Between Stimulus and Response

Years ago, in the book, "7 Habits of Highly Effective People," author Steven Covey shared a concept about "exploring the space between stimulus and response."

Meaning that we would make better decisions if we extended the period between what we think about doing (stimulus) and what we end up choosing to do (response).

100X

Daniel Kahneman also shared the same idea through a metaphor he called the difference between thinking fast and slow. When we think fast, the space between stimulus and response is short, and our decisions are impulsive and don't end up well. But, when we think slowly, we have more time to reflect, and consider the "way" we do things, resulting in better choices.

The principle of 100X is all about taking a pause before responding to our impulses and habits. It makes us stop and ask the 100X question:

> **"How can I do this in a way that will bring me 10X greater return, while using 10X less time, effort, resources, or money (TERM)?"**

From previous chapters, we've already learned that many opportunities to 10X your results exist all around us. As do many opportunities to do things with 10X less TERM.

> **Where those two circles intersect is where we can find the 100X sweet spot, and discover how to do things that will result in 100X results.**

Using the Power of AI to 100X Your Results

But sometimes coming up with answers to our 100X question isn't easy. We know the ideas are out there, but they don't come to mind because we're not used to thinking this way.

It takes a lot of research to identify the abundant ways of doing things that will give us the 100X results we want.

So what do most people do when they want to find more information?

They Google it.

And they search and search, reading article after article. They try to glean as much advice as they can, but it's more like eating fish, picking at the meat while throwing away the bones. And if you've ever eaten fish while trying to avoid the bones, it's not a pleasant experience.

The good news is that AI has come to the rescue by using machine learning algorithms to do the research for us and save us time and money.

And like Prometheus who stole fire from the gods to give to man, AI has been made more commonplace using large language models (LLMs) like ChatGPT (thank you Sam Altman!).

These LLMs scour millions of pieces of data, and do the research for us, saving us hundreds of hours.

Unfortunately, even though ChatGPT has made finding relevant information easier than Google, there is still much work involved.

Like sending out a scout to do reconnaissance on the land you're about to attack, you've got to give the scout (ChatGPT) specific instructions on what to look for.

Meaning you need to put in a lot of effort into prompting ChatGPT with instruction upon instruction, and in teaching it what to look for. Otherwise, you end up with a lot of what you don't need.

100X

Or worse ChatGPT occasionally gives you some random unboned fish, causing you to accidentally swallow a bone (Ouch!).

This comes in the form of "hallucinations", where ChatGPT will put facts together and fabricate information to answer your query, but not knowing that the way it combined the facts is totally incorrect.

This is like a child putting random Lego blocks together, and calling it a castle, and expecting you to live in it—when it obviously looks more like a horse than a castle (and you couldn't live in it anyway).

A Business Browser for ChatGPT

But imagine if you could establish filters that would give ChatGPT specific, preprogrammed instructions that would automatically teach it what to look for.

Kind of like building a ChatGPT browser, which will filter the ChatGPT database so that it only gives you the most relevant, accurate information that you need from just one query.

Or better yet, what if that browser was designed to only give you the most effective business advice that would produce 10X the returns, using 10X less TERM?

Then, instead of having to think and answer the 100X question yourself, you could use this AI business browser to retrieve 100X ideas from ChatGPT's database of billions of pieces of information.

And you can get the 100X answers you need in just one click.

The 100X AI Business Advisor

Well, I found myself in the same situation.

To save myself time and effort thinking of 100X ideas, I decided to build a browser, which would automatically mine all ChatGPT, and only provide 100X answers to business questions.

So no matter what business question it gets asked, it will filter through all the ChatGPT database to only give the highest value, practical and actionable answers that will give me the 10X returns I was looking for, using 10X less TERM.

And to prevent "hallucinations", I uploaded the most effective, vetted, and reliable content for it to base its answers on.

This way, instead of making things up, it would be restricted to answering based on the current, accurate knowledge base, which would ensure its answers are relevant, accurate and current (with no hallucinations).

And with that, the 100X AI Business Advisor was born.

Putting it to Work

Now, I didn't just want this effort to be theoretical. So I put it to the test by using it to build a business from the ground up.

I chose a mobile app company as the first business to build because it was the type of business that would need relevant, current, and up-to-date information to succeed.

100X

Not knowing anything about mobile apps, it was the perfect business to use to put the 100X AI Business Advisor to the test.

I started by asking all the questions a startup would ask. But the most basic was simply, "Give me the entire road map of how to build a successful mobile app company from beginning to the sale of the company, including all the costs and efforts involved."

I didn't have to ask it to give me only the answers that would produce rapid 10X results because it was already programmed to do that. I didn't have to ask it how to do it with 10X less TERM because it already knew to look for that information. I didn't even have to ask it to give me the potential pitfalls and solutions for them because it knew how to find that information for me.

The result? It gave me the entire road map to build a mobile app company, from beginning to end, and the specific steps to take. And the steps it gave me were designed to bypass what everyone else does and get me to the front of the line as soon as possible.

Now the information is great, but you're probably wondering, does it really work?

Well, I took the advice from 100X AI Business Advisor, and asked it every day for more specifics. After putting it to practice for a few weeks, the results were not only mind-blowing to me, but also to my colleagues.

In as little as three months, I was able to build five apps, with two that have already been released, and three more that will be released in the next few months.

And with the help of the 100X AI Business Advisor, I built a brand (100X Entrepreneur's Club), created a monthly newsletter, built a community of tech-savvy, hungry entrepreneurs that want to change the world, and wrote the book you are reading.

So by using AI, and designing it to only give me practical, actionable, and effective advice, the results were 100X more than I could do on my own.

Try the 100X AI Business Advisor for Free

I don't put busines much weight on promises. I am an action-oriented entrepreneur who needs to see things for myself.

So if you're like me, I want to encourage you to try it for yourself. If you already have experience using ChatGPT, it will be easy. Just ask any business question, and it will give you the kind of effective advice that will bring rapid, large-scale results.

And if you are just starting, and don't know the questions to ask, I've added some suggestion questions to the mobile app pertaining to every major area of business to get you started.

So if you want to see an explosion in your business results, and if you want to unlock the power of AI to give you an edge over your competition, and if you want to make a 100X leap toward achieving your business goals, then try the 100X Business Advisor today.

Try the 100X For Free here: 100xbusinessadvisor.ai

100X

Conclusion

The 100X lifestyle is about pausing and asking the 100X question. And by taking the time to ask, you tend to find great opportunities right under your nose.

But even if you can't think of any answers right away to the 100X question, that's ok because now AI is capable of giving you those ideas with just one click.

And if you're tired of spending a lot of time researching on Google, getting generic advice from YouTube, or writing long, detailed, and complex prompts for ChatGPT, then it's time that you tried the 100X AI Business Advisor.

100X AI Business Advisor is the ChatGPT for Business that entrepreneurs have been waiting for. Not only is it easy to use, but it will also give you the effective advice you need that will truly help you go 100X!

So what are you waiting for?

Reach your financial freedom goals today with the power of AI.

Try the 100X Business Advisor for FREE today and supercharge your results by 100X today.

Try it for Free Today on the link below: 100xbusinessadvisor.ai

DID YOU GET VALUE FROM THIS BOOK?

Congratulations on finishing this book!

So, are you ready to go 100X?

If you got a lot of value from this book, then I want to ask you a special favor. Help your other fellow entrepreneurs by leaving a review for this book.

Since a book is judged by its cover, they will need your help to know which books are a good read.

So if you feel like you got a lot of value from this book, please let them know that they should read it too by giving your review.

★ ★ ★ ★ ★

Paperback
If you are reading the paperback, go to Amazon or wherever you bought this book, and leave a review right on the book's page.

eBook
If you are reading on Kindle or E-reader—scroll to the end of the book, and it will prompt a request for review for you.

Thanks again!